SCOTLAND

A HISTORY

8000 B.C. - A.D. 2000

SCOTLAND

A HISTORY

8000 B.C. - A.D. 2000

Fiona Watson

TEMPUS

First published 2001

PUBLISHED IN THE UNITED KINGDOM BY:

Tempus Publishing Ltd
The Mill, Brimscombe Port
Stroud, Gloucestershire GL5 2QG

PUBLISHED IN THE UNITED STATES OF AMERICA BY:

Tempus Publishing Inc.
2 Cumberland Street
Charleston, SC 29401
(Tel: 1-888-313-2665)

Tempus books are available in France, Germany and Belgium
from the following addresses:

Tempus Publishing Group	Tempus Publishing Group	Tempus Publishing Group
21 Avenue de la République	Gustav-Adolf-Straße 3	Place de L'Alma 4/5
37300 Joué-lès-Tours	99084 Erfurt	1200 Brussels
FRANCE	GERMANY	BELGIUM

British Library Cataloguing in Publication Data.
A catalogue record for this book is available from the British Library.

ISBN 0 7524 1796 7

Typesetting and origination by Tempus Publishing.
PRINTED AND BOUND IN GREAT BRITAIN.

For Nick

Who gets me through

Contents

Illustrations

The author and publishers wish to thank the following for permission to reproduce pictures: Alistair Burnett, p.184; John Butcher, p.187 (top); Andrew Cronshaw, p.202 (top); Anthony Duda, p.197 (top); William Hendrie, p.192; J. Husband, p.119; Morag Lloyds, p.194; Patrick Scott, p.173 (bottom); Peter Stewart, p.198; Neil Stirrat, p.187 (bottom); John Swinburne, p.202 (bottom); Anne Watters, p.207 (top).

The pictures on pages 16, 18, 19, 23 (top left), 25, 29, 30, 31 (top), 32, 37 (left and right), 42, 43, 44, 45 (right), 47, 51, 63, 78 (bottom), 87 (top), 95, 98, 99, 100 (left), 105, 109 (bottom), 117, 123, 146, 150, 151, 178, 195 and colour plates 1-21, 23 and 25 are from the author's collection.

All other illustrative material is drawn from the Tempus Archive and the collection of Campbell and Janette McCutcheon.

Acknowledgements

Writing a book like this is an incredibly foolish thing to do, as well as an immensely rewarding one. Professional historians these days are becoming more and more specialised, thanks to the pressures on us to publish more despite having less time to research, which was partly why I wanted to be forced to broaden my reading. But I am very aware of the limitations of my knowledge and owe an immense debt of gratitude to my colleagues who took on the task of going through various sections of the book with a red pen. I know it must have taken a considerable amount of time, that most precious of commodities, and I thank with all my heart Chris Smout, Richard Tipping, Sally Foster and Rod McCullough. I owe an equal debt to two wonderful friends (I think they're still speaking to me), Shona Greig and Maggie Anderson, who read the whole thing to save me from historian-speak, too many long sentences (a bad habit of mine!) and presumptions of knowledge inappropriate for the general reader. Of course, any historical errors, bamboozlingly long sentences and too many 'also's are all my own responsibility.

On a personal note, it has been quite a year – setting up the Centre for Environmental History and Policy at the universities of Stirling and St Andrews, finishing off the television series *In Search of Scotland*, and getting married, as well as writing this book. It has sometimes been rather difficult to see how it could all be done. Jonathan Reeve at Tempus Publishing has done a wonderful job in keeping my nose to the grindstone, while being as flexible as was humanly possible. It was his idea to do the book in the first place, and I am extremely grateful for his sound advice and hard work. I would like to thank the whole team at Tempus who, I know, have worked extremely hard on the book. I owe an especial debt, and perhaps a few drinks, to Tom Cairns in particular, who transformed my manuscript into printable copy with as much care as I would myself (possibly the highest accolade an author can give!), and with astonishing speed.

Finally, I would like to thank my family for their continuing support throughout what was sometimes a rather traumatic time getting the book finished. To mum and dad, who have been as helpful, interested and concerned as one could ever hope parents to be. To Rose and Charlie, our children, who have had to put up with an assault of Scottish history whether they liked it or not, and who have, as a small recompense, found their way into the book's pictures. And last, but not least, to my husband, Nick Hanley, without whom I doubt very much that I would still be sane. I certainly could not have done it without him. I promise now to clear up all the books and bits of paper littering the house and get back to normal.

Thank you so much to you all.

Fiona Watson, December 2000

Preface

The trouble with 'Scotland'

'Scotland' exists – obviously. It exists as a physical reality, a place on a map. But it exists also as a distillation of the accumulated debris left over from its long and supposedly tormented past, the sum of an ever-increasing list of contested component parts.

And so, already, there's more than a hint of trouble. Just as Scotland's future could encompass a wide variety of possibilities, depending on who – and where – you ask, the past is even more of a product of an endless range of distorting mirrors. The *selected* evidence, the events put in and those omitted, the geographical areas chosen as indicative of the 'Scottish' experience at any given time, the personalities given prominence – all these are minefields guaranteed to mislead or give offence despite even the best of intentions.

Admittedly these concerns are not particular to Scotland. Every single one of us who ventures into writing history is a product of any number of prejudices – class, gender, race, to name the most obvious – which inform his or her historical judgements.

So where does that leave anyone foolish enough to try to bring together one single version of Scotland's history? Questions of 'which history?', or even 'whose history?' could reduce the author to a dithering insomniac. Perhaps the most one can do, given the constraints of word limits and the human life span, is to highlight the limitations on the writing of history and the extent to which choices of subject matter have been made to the detriment or even exclusion of other possibilities.

This is important because Scotland's relationship with its larger neighbour and the most influential member of Great Britain – England – is by no means the only, or even the most fundamental, element conditioning Scotland's historical progress. Equally, political concerns, especially those which most easily explain the contemporary situation, are not the whole story either.

Scotland is, and always has been, a complex melting pot of disparate groups, many of which have sat uneasily alongside the mainstream but were equally often at odds with it. The mainstream may not even *necessarily* have represented the views and experiences of sizeable minorities; it has, for example, proved difficult to integrate the activities and outlook of Scottish women into a history of Scotland, and highland history has proved notoriously absent from national history except when it unavoidably impinges on the activities and sensibilities of lowland Scots.

There is no need to immediately leap to conspiracy theories to explain the continuing dominance of the mainstream in Scottish history. In the first place, the subject itself is still comparatively new in any modern sense of the study of history. Indeed, it is only within the last half century that any self-respecting historian would have chosen it as his or her main field of study, for fear of accusations of parochialism from colleagues. So even a basic chronology for the less high-profile periods has been lacking until very recently.

Even more problematic is the irredeemable lack of sources, particularly for any period before about AD 1600. It is, and presumably always will be, impossible to get to grips with anything like a full range of points of view when the written record so often reflects the activities and outlooks of only a tiny minority. Medieval economic Scottish history, for example, will never fully flourish because of this basic constraint and medieval Scottish historians will tend to focus on mainstream politics in order to make the best use of what is available.

Having said that, individual historians are working in less well-documented areas, helping to produce Scottish history from all the angles that historians of more document-productive nations have come to expect. Equally, the scarcity of written evidence has prompted Scottish historians to enlist the help of other disciplines, especially archaeology, a collaboration that is often subsequently pursued as a desirable approach to the past in itself.

And let's not forget that we have a rich legacy in oral history, in more than one language and culture. But this evidence, whether it has been written down, as in Blind Harry's *Wallace*, or can still be heard, as in Radio Scotland's *The Twentieth Century*, should be handled with care, because it needs corroboration from elsewhere just like any other source. Nevertheless, it is a priceless window on the past, affording us often unique glimpses of the thoughts and opinions of broader Scottish society.

The above should, quite rightly, be regarded as a rather long-winded attempt by the author to justify what has made its way into this particular book. It is not an 'academic' piece of work, in the sense that it is mostly neither a product of original research, nor will it delve particularly strenuously into the detailed nitty-gritty of current historical debates. What it will attempt to do is provide a basic and unavoidably selective chronology of the main events and trends, while at the same time indicating where the key areas of controversy lie. If nothing else, this book might prompt the reader to delve more deeply into areas of particular interest and a Further Reading section has been included to aid such a journey.

Scottish history is currently enjoying a Golden Age (and how unusual it is to perceive such a thing at the time of its occurrence!). The thirst for information is quite astounding, reflecting a genuine interest in the subject both at home and abroad. This interest was not created by the two 'Scottish' historical films of the 1990s, *Braveheart* and *Rob Roy*, but they certainly made it fashionable. Scotland's past is big business, whether at the box office, promoting our tourist industry, or boosting university student numbers. The debate about the teaching of Scottish history in Scottish schools has reached the point where it is surely a matter of when, rather than if, all Scottish children will receive a basic grounding in their past.

Ultimately that past must be inclusive, not exclusive, however difficult the task. For modern Scots, no matter what their political persuasion, there must be an awareness of the complexity of what has gone before: don't go wandering into the past if you're looking for truth and certainty; it doesn't exist there any more than it exists in the present. Our predecessors were remarkably sophisticated, in their political transactions, in their social arrangements and in their relationships with outsiders and the environment in which they lived; even historical heroes and villains are all ultimately human, which means they are neither perfect nor irredeemable.

It is also crucial to start at the beginning, or as near the beginning as is reasonable without getting bogged down in any primordial swamps. It's all too easy to neglect to understand fully that human history is fundamentally intertwined with the history of the physical mass of land and waterways that has come to be called Scotland. The changing landscape, with its evolving flora and fauna, conditioned its people just as much as the human population altered the landscape.

Scotland has many histories – as do all nations. It will not be possible, in the following pages, to do justice to them all, but hopefully the reader will come away with a picture of Scotland's past as the sum of its many, many component parts.

ONE

Land, Water, Sky

There is a curious irony about the fact that, for most of Scottish history, there has been no such thing as Scotland. This could, of course, be taken as an academic pronouncement of breathtaking impertinence. But it is important to point out, right at the start, that the fusing together of an extremely mixed group of people living on one particular part of this landmass into a nation of Scots is quite an incredible thing to have happened.

Scotland and its people are certainly not alone in taking a convoluted route towards nationhood and there are many more improbable accidents of history which have forged a sense of common interest and identity among groups of profound ethnic diversity. On the other hand, ethnic similarities are by no means a guarantee of a shared future. But as far as this history is concerned – 10,000 years of human occupation of what is now Scotland – the essential fact remains that only around 10% of it is concerned with the history of the nation itself.

I admit that most of this book will concentrate on the last millennium, for two very simple reasons. Firstly, written evidence, the primary tool of the historian, is pretty much restricted to this period and we simply know most about it. Secondly, to be honest, the history of the nation with which modern Scots identify is what fascinates most people. But it is almost impossible to understand how that nation was shaped into being if we know

Scotland ....

In order not to irritate the reader any more than absolutely necessary, it will be taken for granted that if the term 'Scotland' is used before at least 800 AD it is acting merely as a geographical term with which we are all familiar. Scotland as a concept of nationhood and identity only began to evolve – slowly – after that date.

However, it should be noted that the term 'Scotland' or 'Scottish' are used interchangeably for 'Dal Riata' or 'Dal Riatan' before that date, since the *Scotti* came from Dal Riata.

nothing about the complex history of the people and the land that came before.

Archaeologists and environmental scientists are slowly and painstakingly revealing the rich and varied lifestyles and belief systems of these early peoples and their relationship with the surrounding environment, though there is still much to frustrate a full understanding. Their efforts have revealed a history that is worth knowing for its own sake and there is every reason to include it here. The underlying rock and soil structures, the changing climate, the rise and fall of sea-levels – all these things play a crucial role in explaining the restrictions and possibilities of human activity and you can bet your last groat that our predecessors knew their value.

Right from the arrival of the first transient groups of hunter-gatherer-fishers after the last Ice Age, humans have altered their environment in order to fashion a more secure future out of the resources available to them. Scotland and its people are fundamentally linked and we cannot truly understand the history of one without the other.

Over 10,000 years ago the land now called Scotland began to emerge out of the grip of the last Ice Age. Temperatures had already increased dramatically, causing sea levels to rise as the last of the glaciers began to melt. This was still too inhospitable an environment to be attractive to much life – a landscape of bare mountain peaks and

As the freezing weight of the glaciers disappeared, the land that is now Scotland sprang back into life.

valleys filled with glacier-crushed rubble and tundra grassland. But no matter how barren it might have looked to us, hardy herbs and shrubs like juniper and willow were busy taking root, providing sustenance for animals that liked these vast open spaces and difficult conditions: tough, resilient creatures like mammoth, bison, woolly rhinoceros, giant fallow deer, reindeer and giant elk.

But they didn't have the place to themselves for very long – the climate, the elements, and decaying organic matter were busy moulding and mixing with the rock to create better soils. The plant communities that had made such a brave effort to colonize the bare landscape soon found themselves wilting under soaring temperatures and vacated the lower ground for higher altitudes. New types of vegetation which relished the heat moved in. Birch was the first Scottish tree of this period, arriving in central and eastern Scotland almost immediately and spreading into the north and west within a few centuries. Hazel wasn't far behind, with elm, pine and oak completing the arrival of the main tree species by 6500 BC at the latest. Berries, nuts, leaves and roots were now available in plentiful supply, to add to the other delicacies to be found above ground and in the water.

This dense forest was no place for the great beasts of the icy grasslands and they began to die out; new animal species more at home among trees – wolves, red and roe deer, wild boar, bears, elk, and smaller creatures like voles, shrews and red squirrels – took their places. The skies, rivers and seas too were bursting with the sights, sounds and smells of newcomers – birds, fish, shellfish and sea mammals.

In the meantime, the ice was still melting into the oceans, but sea levels had actually begun to recede. The reason for this is quite extraordinary, even if it makes perfect sense: the land, released from the overpowering pressure of the glaciers, was springing back up. By around 8000 BC it had

---

pre-8000 BC
Last Ice Age ending; sea levels rising; life returns

c.8000 – 7500 BC
Birch arrives; humans and other new species arrive

c.7600 BC
Evidence for peat

c.7550 BC
Sea levels fall; hazel arrives

c.7350 BC
Last evidence for reindeer

c.6840 BC
Sea levels rise

c.6500 BC
Elm & oak arrive

c.5500 BC
Pine arrives in highlands

c.5450 BC
Sea levels fall to current levels

c.4500 BC
First signs of farming

c.3300 BC
Beginning of elm decline

pre-3000 BC
Tree-cover reaches its maximum

c.3000 BC
Far north and islands lose trees

c.2800 BC
Pine advances into far north; more major tree losses elsewhere

c.2400 BC
Tree regeneration in some areas

c.2000 BC
Major pine decline; major tree clearance in south

c.1500 BC
Permanent farming only now normal

c.1200 BC
Obvious soil deterioration & erosion

c.800 BC
Climatic deterioration

c.500 BC
New phase of tree loss, especially in south

Caledonian pine forest.

Among the new species to inhabit the expanding Scots forests were birds of prey like the buzzard (left) and the owl.

emerged free from any lingering ice and the last influx of freezing water had made its way into the oceans, causing them to rise yet again.

This process presented a similar threat to terrestrial life as the effects of global warming today: during the middle centuries of the fourth millennium BC the highlands were almost cut off from the lowlands apart from a nine-mile landbridge. Whales could be seen frolicking in the Forth below the castle rock at Stirling, and the early inhabitants of the area were more than capable of hunting them. With these surges in sea level, the evidence for the first human settlements has probably now been lost. But fragments of these early coastlines are still to be found slightly inland, an intriguing reminder of the power of nature.

Forest, bog and heathland quickly re-established itself. To begin with, human populations had to learn to live alongside whatever environmental conditions they found. But that was a temporary state of affairs because they soon learned how to alter those conditions.

On the other hand, the land's basic potential has always limited what humans have been able to do with it. Some areas, such as the carses of the Forth and Tay with their rich clay soils, are ideal for arable farming, but for much of their history they have proved adept at holding water and attracting an intervening layer of peat, which is no good for farming. Then again, these soils at least have potential. Nearly half of the rest of Scotland was only good for rough grazing.

Modern farmers have the advantage of good drainage and modern technology. But their predecessors might actually have coped better with difficult Scottish conditions. Armed with hand-held spades, their aim was to survive and it didn't matter how long it took, how steep the slope (up to a point), or how many people were needed to work the land. No wonder, then, that they could grow crops in places we would find astonishing.

It would be reprehensible indeed if any discussion of the Scottish environment failed to mention the weather. For the first few thousand years temperatures warmed up nicely and by about 4000 BC the first farmers seem to have enjoyed warmer and drier conditions than we are used to today. Global warming has happened at least once already, but from entirely natural causes. Localized weather systems and particular combinations of weather patterns can have a profound effect on human history, helping to promote disease or help cause harvest failure. There is also some scientific evidence to suggest that, in areas where trees found it difficult to grow anyway, climatic fluctuations could have a very definite effect.

We'll consider the specifically human history in the following chapters. But there's no harm in talking generally about the *homo sapiens* who were about to make their homes here. They were only marginally smaller than us – men tended to be around 5' 5" to 5' 9" and women about 5' to 5' 5". Given the wealth of natural resources at their disposal, they were surely healthier than some of those who came later, but they also suffered from bone diseases like osteoporosis at an early age by our standards. Presumably certain wise folk were revered for their healing abilities. Living with nature was probably a more effective mechanism for survival than trying to fight too hard against it.

The population was tiny. Rough guesstimates of around 10,000 are all that have been hazarded for the overall population in this period – that's about the same as work and

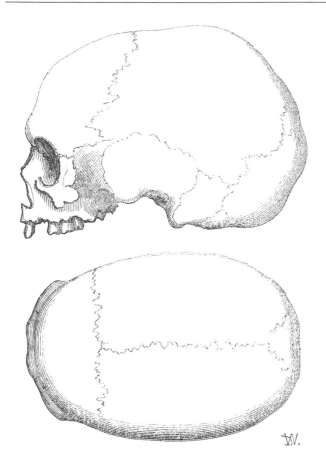

The skull of an early inhabitant of Scotland, from a cist at Cockenzie, East Lothian.

study at my own university campus at Stirling. But it's just as well – each individual needed a good portion of land to sustain a hunter-gatherer-fisher lifestyle.

So, there were considerable pluses and minuses about living in Scotland, just like today. Natural resources were available in abundance, though exactly what they were varied from place to place. Overall environmental conditions were not static either and in the earliest years there was a considerable amount of readjustment going on as the land, rivers and seas, not to mention the climate itself, settled down to life without ice. It's difficult to imagine what this prehistoric landscape would have looked like to the earliest settlers – there's certainly nothing left of it now. So, we begin this history of Scotland with a fairly blank page, but with plenty of undiscovered potential.

TWO

Settlers and Invaders

8000 – c.2500 BC

If you go to southern England these days, you can't help noticing how many people there are, crammed into every available space, creating an almost totally 'lived-in' landscape. Although the Scottish central belt has gone much the same way, the north and west of the country is renowned for its awesome, empty spaces. But this is much more a reaction to the overcrowding going on elsewhere than an accurate reflection of the pristine nature of Scotland's so-called wildernesses. Though these areas now seem formidably remote and difficult for humans to live in, they have, in fact, sustained communities in both the recent and far distant past.

The Mesolithic (c.8000 BC – c.4000 BC)

People had almost certainly found their way into Scotland in previous interglacials – the British Isles have, after all, been occupied off and on for a staggering 500,000 years – but any trace of these earliest settlers has either eroded away or not yet been found. Soon after the end of the last Ice Age people began to think of looking for fresh places to find food in the north. Britain was still linked with Europe via a landbridge until the seas finally absorbed it around 6000-5000 BC so people could walk straight across from the Continent as well as coming up from southern Britain.

These early adventurers were nomadic – the few traces left of them indicate that they lived in temporary camps made of timber and skins, as well as the caves which had long provided shelter for early humans. When they came across a sheltered spot, they would surely have been delighted with what they found – an impressive array of accessible food sources: nuts, berries, seeds, roots and fungi, fish, seabirds and shellfish, and all sorts of animals to gather and hunt.

After this first phase of opportunistic and transitory occupation, these visitors would start to feel more at home and able to think seriously about systematically using these abundant resources. There were now many more people, spread out across the land, but temporary camps were still the norm, as life was spent largely on the move. As the seasons changed, the group moved on to the next spot where they expected to find a good yield of other things.

The most likely final stage in this process was probably the development of a system of semi-permanent settlements, combined with temporary work camps. The former would be inhabited mainly by the slow moving – old people and children and their carers. Those with particular jobs to do might also stay behind to get on with their work in peace, though no-one was excused from hunting and gathering. The younger and stronger people then moved out of the claustrophobic company of their elder relatives and young siblings to hunt in the hills, returning to the main camp with supplies as colder weather approached. Women were just as much a part of these teams as men, with the main responsibility for processing animal carcasses into usable commodities: dried meat, fur for wearing and using in the home, fat for tallow, gut for bow strings, bone and antlers for tools.

Though the concept of ownership didn't really exist, each community possibly had rights over particular resources at certain times of the year. These early people ranged over surprising distances in log canoes or coracles – one such stamping ground seems to have encompassed Islay and Jura with the smaller surrounding islands and the mainland opposite. They were equipped with the defining tool of the Mesolithic – the microlith, a tiny serrated stone blade embedded in a wooden shaft. Though presumably used for hunting, it had a range of other uses, while equipment like bows, arrows and spears, together with nets and lines were also needed to catch the range of sea and land creatures that made up the Mesolithic diet. People certainly ate well.

There have been stereotypes aplenty for these early settlers – from savages, noble or otherwise, to wise hippy-types living in perfect harmony with their environment. It is true that such a lifestyle did little, comparatively speaking, to affect the landscape and other living things. Hunter-gatherer-fishers chose and adapted their way of life to make the most of what they found. But the evidence also suggests that they were willing to change things where they could.

Despite the difficulties of relying almost entirely on what nature produced, this lifestyle had its attractions. There was a limit to the amount of work to be done, leaving quite a lot of spare time. Some form of group identity almost certainly existed. Each group would

Mushrooms were just part of the bounty of food readily
available to early inhabitants.

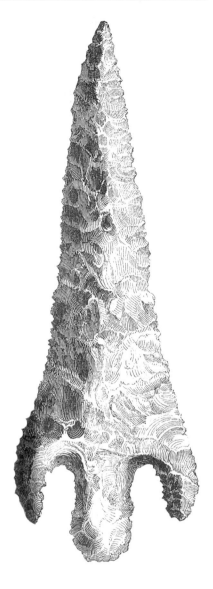

Typical of the knapped stone blades used for a variety of
purposes in Mesolithic Scotland, this flint arrowhead was
found on the island of Skye.

Some of the more characteristic varieties of stone hammers
and axes found in Scotland.

have their own way of doing things, their own defining symbols that marked them out from others.

Strangers arriving in occupied areas were no doubt regarded with suspicion, given the limits to the numbers of people a hunter-gatherer-fisher lifestyle could support. However, population pressure does not seem to have been a huge problem in this period, and newcomers could still presumably be directed elsewhere.

Contacts with other groups must also have been important, and not just for trade. Days of feasting and gift-giving would help to past the time and provide the sense of solidarity and security of being part of a larger community. When young people were looking for partners, it was essential that the gene pool be expanded beyond the immediate group and doubtless these events carried the added frisson of potential romantic success for the unattached. (Though such encounters had to be conducted without the aid of alcohol!) Swapping ideas and stories was also important, to emphasise existing links and help develop new techniques and strategies. Thanks to these links, a major new way of life started to attract the attention of the Mesolithic people by 4000 BC.

The early Neolithic (*c*.4000 BC – *c*.2000 BC)

As communities got bigger and more organized, efforts were made to bring the woods that dominated the landscape under some control. These early peoples knew how to **coppice** and **pollard** to encourage new branches to grow back straight (very useful for making things with) and to produce bigger harvests of hazelnuts. Selected patches of wood may even have been set on fire to create clearings which would attract animals like deer, making them easier to kill.

This was a complex society, where behaviour was governed by an evolving set of rules that made perfect sense for the environment in which people lived and what was available to them. But life was more than just a struggle to bring in enough food.

The lack of evidence for buildings and objects used for work, play and ritual activity means that archaeologists have little to go on to understand much beyond the most basic patterns of life. But there are a few hints. Skeletal remains from other countries indicate that close family relationships – mother and child, husband and wife – were recognized and respected in death, and therefore in life too. Particular animals or birds were probably used as symbols of the group, a practice that continued well beyond the Mesolithic.

The adoption of a farming lifestyle, with its permanent villages and field-systems, was tremendously important in the evolution of human society. What happened in Scotland was distinctive, a reflection of the particular geological, environmental and social/cultural factors already at work. But it was most certainly not 'Scottish'. The

> **Coppicing:**
>
> involves cutting the branches of young trees near the ground.
>
> **Pollarding:**
>
> basically the same but the branches are cut higher up, usually to stop animals grazing the vulnerable shoots.

A coppiced hazel.

regional diversity that was a likely feature even of the nomadic lifestyle of Mesolithic peoples now came to flourish as they slowly settled down. The ownership of land, even if it is held communally, naturally leads its settlers to feel possessive about it.

Farming – basically the cultivation of domesticated cereal crops and animals – began in the Near East, around modern-day Iraq. By about 6500 BC the new system had reached the Mediterranean and over the following millennia knowledge worked its way slowly north. We are not talking about an overnight conversion to the idea that the current lifestyle would just no longer do – farming is, after all, extremely hard work. Indeed, some argue that permanently settled farming communities didn't become the norm until around 2000 BC.

It is also quite unfashionable to conclude that wheat- and sheep-brandishing invaders must have taken over the British Isles, forcing the native populations to adopt their way of life, though we certainly used to believe that conquest must have preceded the change. While farmers may well have migrated north, just as the early settlers had done, it is equally likely that contact with Continental practitioners brought about a gradual adoption of the attractive aspects of farming by the natives. What probably appealed most was the ability to generate a more reliable and varied source of food and raw materials.

It now became feasible to invest resources and energy into building more long-lasting and substantial structures, though, to be honest, the early Neolithic is served far better – in terms of archaeological remains – by buildings dedicated to the dead than to the living. Archaeologists are very keen to stress that the pattern of survival should not blind us to the rich variety of building types. For example, though stone structures have survived comparatively well and in such large numbers, they are by no means the whole story; timber buildings whose existence is hinted at in crop marks were probably far more common. And no matter what the building material, there were different models to choose from.

But, while it is dangerous to generalize, the people of the early Neolithic quite often lived in small rectangular houses, emphasizing the individual family unit. One of the earliest farmsteads is at Knap of Howar on Papa Westray (*c.*3400 BC), built snugly into the ground, presumably in an attempt to protect itself from the winds now unhindered by trees in the far north (see below). Balbridie in Aberdeenshire (*c.*3800 BC) is the site of a much larger timber hut similar to Continental structures, though it may have been used for a communal purpose rather than as a family house. Practicalities played their part, but fashion, imagination and contact with others also had an impact.

By around 3000 BC we see the first villages emerging, such as at Skara Brae. Like Knap of Howar, the buildings are squat unremarkable stone constructions from the outside, again reflecting environmental conditions. The low internal passageway system also provided shelter from the elements when nipping from house to house. Timber-based settlements in more sheltered wooded areas were presumably organized rather differently but have tended not to survive. These village sites were usually enclosed – another new phenomenon – though probably not for defence. Such banks or fences perhaps underlined the settlement's physical presence – an oasis of human control in the midst of a powerful, capricious natural world.

Internally, however, Skara Brae illustrates just how sophisticated these people were. Though the houses were packed together, each family could bar the door to their own

A view of the Stone Age village at Skara Brae, Orkney.

The interior of a house at Skara Brae, with the distinctive stone dresser facing the entrance.

homes *from the inside*. It would be tempting to put this down to fear and insecurity, but I prefer to imagine that, like their Mesolithic predecessors, they appreciated the limitations of communal living, as well as its benefits.

If, however, you were a welcome guest and invited to duck through the passage into the house, the first sight to greet you would be the stone dresser strategically placed, and presumably adorned with treasured possessions, opposite the door. The residents also had a central hearth and possibly their own inside toilets – not bad for over 5000 years ago. True, there wasn't much room inside – no separate living and sleeping quarters – but even if the individual wasn't catered for, there was plenty of scope to nurture the family as well as the group.

As with other sites, not all the houses were living quarters – at least one building was most likely a workroom or store. Considering that Skara Brae was occupied for around 500 years, each generation presumably had its own ideas about how the interiors should be organized and what sort of activities needed accommodation. Crafts such as carpentry and stone-working were becoming highly skilled, judging by the range and types of tools used. Pottery making, associated with the arrival of farming, may well have been practised locally, though trade also brought the newest samples to all parts of Scotland. They needed something to put on the dressers after all.

However, the vast majority, if not every able-bodied person, would still be involved in the fundamental job of producing enough for their community to live on throughout the year. Hunting, fishing and gathering berries, roots and other available goodies were still part of the annual cycle, but now the surrounding land was also controlled, managed and regularly exploited.

Plenty of storage space at Skara Brae.

Pottery urns from a grave at Banchory, probably created for domestic use.

Stone urn from the Hill of Knowth in the county of Meath.

Farming had very definite implications for Scotland and its environment, especially its forest cover. But then again climatic change was also having an impact – the mild temperatures of the post-glacial period were giving way to cooler conditions and by around 3000 BC trees found it very difficult to grow in the far north and the islands. Woods were thinning out elsewhere too and gaps in the cover may have been at least partly natural in origin. The growth of peat bogs is also associated with wetter, cooler temperatures.

The density of prehistoric woods causes much argument, as does the contribution of farming to their decline. There is no agreement, for example, on the cause of a huge wipeout of elm trees noticeable from around 4000 BC. Some argue that an outbreak of disease similar to the late-twentieth-century century epidemic was responsible; others point to the widespread practice of feeding cattle their favourite elm leaves as a more likely cause of such a consistent decline without the benefit of modern transport systems to help spread disease. Pollen scientists may have found evidence for soil erosion,

An ancient herb garden would have provided both culinary and medicinal plants.

often caused by the removal of trees. But the implications of that – up to and including the abandonment of settlements – are hotly debated. Nevertheless, humans were now making a very definite impact on the environment.

There's no doubt, for example, that fields for planting crops and keeping animals required the deliberate felling of huge swathes of woodland. A stone axe could deal with a small to moderate-sized tree; fire, or bark stripping, could kill off bigger specimens. The Neolithic farmer might then have used hoes and spades or a basic plough (an ard) to scratch through the soil. The harvest would then be placed on a flat stone (a quern) and

Grinding corn the hard way.

roughly ground by hand with another smaller rock. The results could be made into bread or a porridge-type concoction, and also distilled into alcohol.

Unfortunately, the new farmer didn't necessarily go through the whole clearing-tilling process only once. He may have rotated his crops and used some kind of fertilizer, such as seaweed, to make the land more productive. But if not, his fields would run out of nutrients every six years or so, and he would require more land. Though the original fields could be used again a few years later, it's easy to see why, even under this more settled system, a tiny population needed a larger and larger area of land to live on.

Fields for crops require some sort of definition, anything from basic hurdle fences to rocks and boulders, transforming the landscape further. But pastoral farming also required field boundaries, though grazing animals are happy browsing in woods. Hungry mouths and the pressure of feet soon turn a plain or slope of woodland shrubs and plants into grassland. Given the long tradition in Scotland of moving animals up and down the hills with the seasons, the lack of archaeological evidence for **transhumance** is surprising – cattle, sheep and goats could all be moved uphill, though pigs probably couldn't. However, some would argue that the beautiful and enigmatic cup and ring marks gouged into rocks indicate boundaries and routes related to summer grazing.

The population probably started to increase, not least because babies surely survived better on this mushy new diet of cereals and milk, while adults

> **Transhumance:**
>
> the practice of taking animals from lower slopes, where they spent the winter, up into the hills for the summer. Those who tended these flocks stayed up there in temporary structures later called shielings

*Highland wooded
pasture.*

*Prehistoric cup and ring
marks, thought by some
to delineate boundaries
and routes connected
with summer grazing.*

31

Pork provided vital protein to Neolithic man.

would also have benefited from the proteins, vitamins, minerals and fat to be found in eggs, milk, cheese, and grains. Surplus crops and animals could be traded, providing opportunities to acquire luxury goods. This increasingly settled farming lifestyle also gave its practitioners more chance to express their beliefs about life, and, more particularly, death.

The sacred ritual sites associated with the Neolithic are the most obvious legacy of the entire period. Farming certainly seems to have inspired people to make their mark on the landscape for purely symbolic purposes. One of the earliest ceremonial sites (*c*.3500 BC) is the Cleaven Dyke in Perthshire, which, when it was finally completed, formed a bank with ditches $1\frac{1}{2}$ miles long. Even though it probably wasn't built in one go, this was quite an achievement. But although **cursus monuments** like the Cleaven Dyke were used as burial sites, their main function was ceremonial. Communal tombs were more usually built as places for the dead.

When a person died, he or she would probably be left out on a raised platform till the flesh had been removed from the body in a process known as excarnation. This practice is still observed in some parts of the world today and may reflect a belief in the need to set the spirit free from its decaying outer shell. Once the skeleton had been fully exposed, it

> **Cursus monuments:**
>
> though there's no connection, these were named from the Latin *cursus*, because they were originally thought to be the remains of Roman chariot-racing circuits.

was ready to join its ancestors in the burial monument. The precise form of these tombs probably reflected regional tastes and trends just like houses for the living: for example, the north and west tended to build in stone, the south and east in less durable materials. But they all performed a similar function – to maintain the community in the afterlife and, equally importantly, to underline the connection between that community and its land.

These tombs required considerable communal effort to build, whether in stone or timber. There doesn't seem to have been any age or gender distinction in who was buried

The megalithic tomb at Bonnington Mains, known locally as the Witch's Stone.

Another famous Scottish cromlech, the Auld Wives' Lift in Stirlingshire.

there, though the number of recovered skeletons can't add up to the total population, suggesting that not everyone was admitted to the communal tombs after death. Presumably the tribal elders presided over the regular ceremonial events requiring the blessing of the ancestors but their status reflected respect rather than a formal hierarchy.

The first 3000 years or so of human occupation of Scotland after the last Ice Age are very difficult to get to grips with in any detail. But it is possible to catch a glimpse of these early settlers at work and play. These people were clearly not savages, but adaptable, intelligent colonizers of what was still a difficult environment of unpredictable conditions and dangerous predators. The family played a fundamental role in social relations, though we know practically nothing beyond its obvious significance. A tribal identity also seems to have been important, even when lifestyles were still more or less nomadic.

It is tempting to make too much of the significance of the introduction of farming – change took place over several millennia, different things were happening in different places at different times and we should not think of these people as fully settled until the end of the early Neolithic. Nevertheless, the increasing association of a people with a particular territory seems to have unleashed a desire to make a much greater mark on the landscape, to tell the wider world who lived there and what they believed in. On a more practical level, the wider range of goods now being produced, from alcohol to pottery, must have stimulated trade and given the economy a boost. The early peoples of 'Scotland' seem to have got off to a good start.

THREE

Land and Community
*c.*2500 BC – AD 80

The later Neolithic way of life some 4500 years ago was probably basically familiar to earlier communities – the agricultural cycle does not seem to have fundamentally changed, for example, though there was certainly some innovation. But in other ways the peoples of the later Neolithic through into the Iron Age operated rather differently from their predecessors.

Once communities finally settled down, they could express their thoughts about the world they lived in and their place within it. This world did not just include the immediate environment, but encompassed the very heavens themselves. The mysteries of the universe had probably always been contemplated, but now the settled lifestyle provided more opportunity for some sort of formal definition. Those individuals or groups who proved particularly adept at explaining and controlling such mysteries might also acquire more power. And once that had happened, there was nothing to stop all sorts of changes in social and economic organization. This was a long drawn-out process, though, and certainly not uniform across the land.

In the later Neolithic, the most striking innovation was a desire to set apart particular members of the community by giving them select access to ritual sites and tombs. In some places, an effort seems to have been made to exclude people from even seeing into the ritual site – which often included the earlier communal tomb – by building a bank with an inner ditch around it. These are known as henges. Huge stone or timber uprights were often a new feature of the inner sanctum and though they could be seen from afar, the ceremonies taking place inside were safely hidden. Though we don't know exactly what the participants got up to in these sacred places, feasting and sacrifice (predominantly, but not exclusively, of animals) probably formed part of it, as had been the case with the earlier communal monuments.

However, given the evidence for social norms among the living (see below), we should probably keep an open mind about whether or not a hierarchy now existed within the community itself. Though some of these henges and certainly the tombs are only big enough for a few select members of the community to squeeze into at any one time, the communal burial vaults, like the Tomb of the Eagles on Orkney, were often no bigger. Perhaps we just don't find it easy to understand peoples for whom leadership can be accommodated without the acquisition of power and wealth and the creation of a social elite, though there are examples, such as among native American tribes, from our own time.

The later Neolithic tombs are nevertheless a very interesting departure from earlier burial practice, because now many communities clearly wished to acknowledge the importance of certain key members by giving them an individual burial place. One of the most splendid surviving examples is at Maes Howe on Orkney, which, like other ritual places, seems to have been designed to align with particular annual events in the sky, in this case the winter solstice. Doubtless to observers this relationship was also a symbol of great power. What makes the site even more special is its proximity to the complementary henges at Stenness and the Ring of Brodgar. This was a landscape of profound ritual

The great burial mound at Maes Howe on Orkney.

*Clockwise from left: the
entrance tunnel at Maes
Howe; standing stones at
Stenness, Orkney; one of
the giant uprights at
Stenness; the picturesque
stones at Lundin.*

The famous standing stones at Callanish, Stornoway.

significance and those buried at Maes Howe presumably once played a crucial role in what happened there.

But the evidence for domestic life, including the settlement at Barnhouse on Orkney which was probably associated with these three sites, gives no indication that such important individuals lived in distinctive houses, as we might expect. At Barnhouse, there is a larger building which looks as if it certainly could have accommodated a chiefly family, but not everyone agrees that this was its function. Even more intriguingly, Skara Brae was probably built slightly later than Barnhouse and, as we've seen, its layout strongly suggests that an integrated community lived there. The one building at Skara Brae that appears separate or different seems to have been used as a workshop, as may be the case at Barnhouse.

The family probably remained the most fundamental social unit, but whether or not they lived in individual farmsteads or compact villages, co-operation and the bond of the community was the driving force of both everyday farming life and special ceremonial activity. Surpluses were produced in good years, to be traded for goods from all over the British Isles and even the Continent.

But local identities were important too and what seems to be the case in one part of the country most definitely cannot automatically be applied to another. This is just as true for ritual sites – recumbent stone circles, where one mighty stone lies flat among the other uprights, are only found in the north-east, for example – and we can assume that the rituals and belief systems themselves were just as varied.

Tensions undoubtedly existed within and among the various tribes even before the emergence of a hierarchy. But settlement sites were not built to be defended so any violence was presumably not completely endemic, as we sometimes presume. However, the discovery of metal and the development of the skills to mould objects of great beauty and killing power were soon to bring about more change. It also made the acquisition of power and resources in the hands of a few a much easier proposition.

The Age of Metal (c.2500 BC – AD200)

The third millennium BC witnessed more significant change, particularly the introduction of metalworking, based on copper, then gold, then bronze, to Scotland. But the overall trends in the way people lived and died indicate that most things continued as they had done in the Neolithic and it wouldn't serve any useful purpose to be too dogmatic about where the Neolithic ends and the Bronze Age begins.

Again, it's not clear where the impetus for such innovation came from – perhaps there was a new wave of emigration pushing settlers already practised in metalworking further north, or else the technique migrated through contacts with such craftsmen. But once the skills had arrived, regular trading links with elsewhere became even more imperative for the simple reason that bronze is made out of copper, which is found naturally in Scotland, and tin, which is not.

To produce raw copper, these prehistoric craftsmen had to heat the ore to a tremendous temperature (over 1000° C) in a little furnace. Charcoal was the only available material to

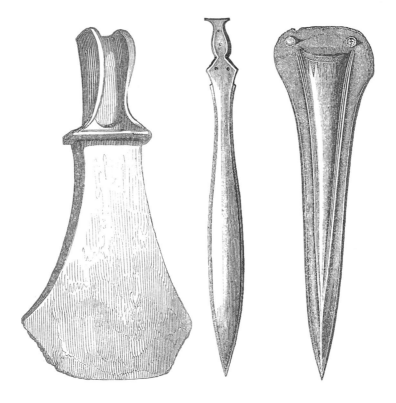

A selection of bronze artifacts. From left: a Bronze Age palstave, fastened to a straight wooden handle to serve as a spade, crowbar or pickaxe; leaf-shaped sword found at Arthur's Seat; dagger from Pitcaithly, Perthshire.

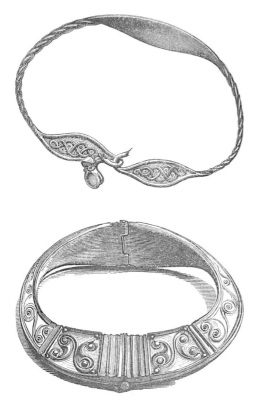

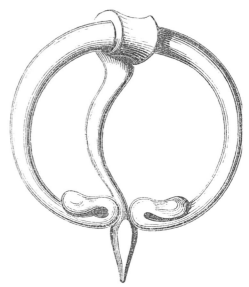

Above: Bronze ring fibula found at Granton, Midlothian.

Above left: Bronze head-ring found at Clunemore.

Left: Head-ring or diadem from the village of Stichel, Roxburghshire.

provide such high heat and finding charcoal deposits is therefore a clue to early settlements engaging in this kind of activity. Gold was also to be found in the Scottish hills, but most of the beautiful gold objects from this period actually came from Ireland.

The ability to mould the shape of these hard and beautiful substances led, of course, to the making of weapons, as well as tools. But many of the surviving intricate and delicate objects of war were probably used more for ceremonial purposes rather than in anger. The real value of this new craft was in the provision of the most exquisite decorative goods.

There was a price to be paid for such luxuries, in more ways than one. Now there were extremely obvious ways of marking people's social status because such high quality craftsmanship was not to be worn by just anyone. And once this kind of social shift had taken place, there was a growing incentive for the elite to maintain itself by seeking to control more and more of the surplus needed for trade.

Social status was still a primary factor in the form of burial too. The most common sacred sites for the Bronze Age were the stone circles, which, as we've seen, began to appear in the later Neolithic. The individual burial sites were now firmly integrated into the wider landscape, incorporating other, often older, sacred sites, a clear indication that calling on the authority of the past was vitally important to people then, as it is to us now.

Cinerary urns from Memsie and Ratho. The larger of the two was found beside a broken bronze sword.

It is not yet clear that the scale of these ritual landscapes implies that the societies constructing them were run by an elite which alone could organize the necessary labour – tribal elders might be just as capable of managing such projects if the community as a whole approved of the end result. On the other hand, it is true that children were also buried in these important tombs, including Maes Howe. Was there now an elite based on blood? If so, this was another major shift in social values.

However, this rather begs the question as to what happened after death to the 'ordinary' people without whom these great burial sites could not have been built. The answer, as ever, is not simple, but might involve a range of possibilities, including, in this period, cremation and burial of the ashes in various types of pottery. Once again we must acknowledge the range of ways in which different groups chose to differentiate themselves both from contemporaries and their own predecessors over and above particular architectural styles. As well as using their own tribal symbols, they could, for example, acknowledge the importance of particular occupations by burying a practitioner with the articles associated with his or her job. Pollen evidence suggests, for example, that by the Bronze Age the plant meadowsweet may have been placed in graves, a rare and revealing insight into the sensibilities of early settlers.

Meadowsweet seems to have been important to the Mesolithic population, pollen evidence suggesting that it was placed in graves.

The Bronze Age seems to have coincided with a noticeable increase in population, judging from the fact that settlements now appeared on less desirable land such as hillsides. Round houses were fairly common, in contrast to the rectangular buildings favoured earlier. By the later second millennium BC there is also evidence for a new type of settlement – huts built on unenclosed platforms into the hills (though, as ever, his is certainly not a universal phenomenon). This move into the uplands and other less easily cultivated areas indicates that better land was now almost entirely used up. This may be backed up by the fact that the third millennium seems to have witnessed a new phase of tree clearance, perhaps to provide more land for planting crops or grazing livestock.

Those who had been forced to settle on more marginal land were extremely vulnerable to potential stresses, environmental or otherwise. These included a deteriorating climate, human-made soil erosion and, perhaps, Icelandic volcanic eruptions throwing debris into the atmosphere, all of which might comine to force communities off the hills. It is impossible, of course, to point to one single cause. But the essential point is that those caught out on the margins had to go somewhere, and this may have spelled trouble for those living on more fertile land.

In the years after 1000 BC, the climate did indeed decline, perhaps helping to encourage just such an exodus and persuade those lucky enough to be able to stay put of the need to defend themselves. But what is more striking about the late Iron Age (*c*.500 BC) is, in fact, the rich diversity and sophistication of settlement types, not all of which were defensible but which certainly seemed to form definite regional patterns.

The huge burial chambers accommodating only very select members of the community were a thing of the past – the concern now was very much with the living, and resources and energy were poured into houses rather than tombs. Individual farmsteads were still a common enough phenomenon. But where people did live together, after 1000 BC, open settlements tended to give way to villages surrounded by some form of enclosure with, usually, a single entrance.

An exodus from the hills makes a handy explanation for such apparent defensiveness. But at the same time hillforts emerged as a settlement type prevalent in southern and eastern Scotland, which makes no sense at all if such an exodus was a general occurrence. Then again, climate change affects different parts of Scotland differently and retreat from the margins didn't necessarily happen everywhere – the south and east were far less vulnerable than the north and west.

This move *into* the hills in the south and east may indeed indicate the increasing dominance of particular groups – why not take hold of the uplands as well, so that crop production could be complemented by keeping large numbers of animals on what were effectively ranches? And since a hillfort's position means that it can be seen from afar, why not make it as impressive as possible and part of the ritual landscape? Incredible as it might seem, hill settlements in general had the potential to accommodate huge numbers of people – Eildon Hill North in the Borders, for example, could have housed between 3000

A reconstructed thatched house similar to those in Iron Age villages.

Large timbers were used to form the frames of houses (above) while wattle and daub was probably the usual form of walling (left, below).

and 6000 individuals. But given these hill forts' exposure to the elements and distance from the arable fields which presumably fed their inhabitants, it has been suggested that these were not permanently settled but acted as important focal points, as seats of government, or for special ceremonies or trading extravaganzas at particular times. The walls were probably there, then, primarily for show, not defence, though they could presumably be used for that if necessary.

In the northern and western coastal areas, the most distinctive form of architecture emerging in this period was the brochs, though they were descendants of earlier roundhouses. Again, given the resources needed to build such structures, this may be evidence of increased centralization, although, unlike some of the hill settlements, brochs can't actually accommodate that many people (perhaps around thirty). Despite the high walls, the primary living areas seem to have been confined to the ground or first floor, with

An imposing broch tower on the isle of Lismore.

A broch at Glenelg.

animals often sharing the space. These distinctive and lofty buildings certainly look as if theywere the homes of important leaders and their families, and probably were. Some brochs, like that at Gurness on Orkney, now have the remains of villages surrounding them, but, as we shall see, these villages were built much later than the brochs.

In the centuries leading up to the birth of Christ, brochs seem to have been replaced by wheelhouses, another architectural type characteristic of these exposed coasts. These weren't as tall as the brochs, meaning that they weren't so impressive outside. But inside their builders have provided showpieces for their skills in drystane dyking, constructing a series of curved pillars parallel and partly attached to the circular outer wall and supporting the stone outer edge of the roof – hence the name, wheelhouse.

By the later Iron Age, it seems likely that distinctive power blocs based in Shetland and Caithness centred themselves on particular brochs, which may indeed have acted as homes to men best described as kings. Although they seem to date from slightly later, the wheelhouses perhaps came into use to distinguish important families from those both above and below them in the social order. And though we might regard these areas as isolated and remote today, the admittedly scarce evidence does seem to indicate surprisingly vibrant connections with other parts of Britain and Europe in terms of trade and diplomacy.

The people of these coastal areas faced particular problems with environmental change, as they became more exposed to colder, wetter weather and, more particularly, the **advance of peat**. They could still farm crops, but animals, both husbanded and hunted, were at least as important to their economy. In more temperate areas, however, the evidence for field systems suggests that the growing of crops was the main farming activity and pushed to the limits of capacity.

The evidence of souterrains – underground passages attached to houses – may back this up. Though the jury is still out on exactly what role they played in the Iron Age economy, the theory that they might have been used for storage would imply a huge surplus of foodstuffs being generated in the south and east particularly. The fact that souterrains were found all over these areas and were attached to ordinary houses also implies that the community as a whole, rather than just an elite, still controlled this surplus.

Increasingly complex interiors, providing smaller, more private, spaces, suggest that particular members of the family now had their own space, though the hearth tended to act as the focal point. But beyond these basics, we're still not sure how exactly people organized themselves. Roman writers suggest that polygamy was practised but we should not automatically believe them since the native peoples of Scotland were, after all, enemies of Rome and basically portrayed as painted savages, a view that is, to put it charitably, extremely prejudiced.

We know so much more about how Iron Age people lived simply because the evidence is much thicker on the ground. And one of the main reasons for that is the growing tendency to use stone instead of wood, perhaps as a response to more unpleasant

---

The advance of peat

Peat advances for four main reasons - changes in the soil, climate decline, burning and tree clearance. It seems to have begun c.7600 BC, but it is very difficult to plot its expansion, and explain why it did so.

Reconstructed crannog on Loch Tay.

climatic conditions but possibly also reflecting a growing lack of timber. Pollen evidence strongly suggests that 500 BC heralded yet another great push into the trees, perhaps on a hitherto unprecedented scale. Again, this may have been because population was on the increase. But perhaps we are also seeing the results of a greater ability to organize on a larger scale, thanks to increasing centralization.

One obvious exception to building in stone were the crannogs, a building-type reasonably common in Scotland, especially the highlands and south-west, and also to be found in Ireland and, to a limited extent, Wales. In essence, crannogs were wooden roundhouses constructed over water and usually linked to the bank by a causeway of some kind. It is not entirely clear why their inhabitants would want to live on a windy, exposed loch though some argue that it was to avoid using up good agricultural land for siting the village. Also, as the reconstructed crannog near Kenmore in Perthshire vividly demonstrates, you make far more of an impact there than on land and the crannogs may represent important local centres rather like the hill forts, which were also designed to impress.

Taken altogether, the increasingly helpful evidence from surviving settlements reinforces the need for caution in attempting to take a Scottish approach to the whole prehistoric period. Varying climates, environmental conditions, external contacts – to name but a few contributory factors – all merged together to mould very different economic, social and political systems, which found visual expression in different types of architecture, settlement patterns, possessions and physical appearance, again to name but a few. In some areas there might well have been a need to defend home, farm and village, but elsewhere there was no lack of stability and security and the primary emphasis was on underlining the authority and power of key groups and, eventually, their leaders.

Any hierarchy was also complex – many stone roundhouses, for example, were sufficiently impressive to have housed substantial farmers who were members of the landowning classes but not necessarily on the top rung. It is likely that the houses of the least well-off would also be the least durable, making it inevitable, as is so often the case in history, that their voices will continue to remain virtually unheard in history. But, as with later times, these 'ordinary' people would be the main labourers, and, in times of crisis, the soldiers; without them there would be no surpluses and no ability to take over new territory or defend the existing one.

And the means to make a forcible takeover bid was certainly to hand. Iron is a much more durable metal than bronze and so any iron weapons were likely to be much more effective. Bog iron, from which the ore was smelted, was commonly available throughout Scotland. The raw iron was then moulded into the correct shape while it was still extremely hot. All of these processes involved considerable skill and, as with the intricate bronze objects, they were almost certainly made by specialist craftsmen.

Presumably the ability to make such weapons, together with forms of armour to protect both the soldier and his horse, might well have encouraged some tribes to become more militaristic. The evidence before the Roman invasion does not indicate any serious and long-term degeneration into warfare – if there had been such a development, then this would surely have been reflected in the design of buildings and settlements. Sporadic fighting must certainly have occurred but there was still no need to make a way of life out of warfare: wearing a weapon was at least as much about displaying power and prestige as intending to inflict damage. On the other hand, it would be foolish to pretend that this society hadn't started to divide into potentially warring entities as larger regional idebtities became stronger.

Technology advanced in other ways too. By the time iron became available in Scotland, the wheel had also made it this far north, meaning that carts and chariots could make much lighter work of all sorts of activities (though going by boat would still be preferable to trying to negotiate early roads). The horse seems to have become far more important in the Iron Age, making communications easier and quicker. If increased centralization was indeed taking place, then the ability to move relatively quickly over land was surely vital to maintaining authority over a larger area. Last, but by no means least, the introduction of the rotary quern made life easier – no more gruelling hours spent forcing the grain to split by hand using a small rock. Now an upper circular stone was placed on top of the lower one, with a hole in the middle to pour the grain down, and it was just a question of turning the upper one and waiting for the refined grain to flow out. Since the grain grinders may well have been women, it is tempting to imagine that the introduction of this piece of home technology was as welcome as the washing machine in more recent times!

The importance of communal activities such as story-telling, feasting and having a good time, not to mention showing off to the opposite sex, was still a fundamental part of

The horse became more common in Scotland during the Iron Age, facilitating communication and transport across a wider area.

A more sophisticated variant of the rotary quern was the pot quern, such as this one found in East Lothian. The central millstone, rotated in the pot to grind cereals fed through the hole in the top, originally had a handle on each side. The metal ring is a modern addition.

prehistoric life. Without the benefit of ritual and burial sites, it is difficult to say much about the development of thought and belief, but there are some hints to the spiritual life of these early Scots. Peoples of the later prehistoric period had developed a complex relationship with that most fickle of deities, Nature. Any spiritual system which seeks to understand and control such unpredictable forces as the weather and the occurrence of disease was bound to lead to attitudes and behaviour that we might find bizarre, not to mention deeply violent. Nevertheless, it is only human nature to try to understand the mysteries of the universe and, considering how much of life for these people must have seemed quite inexplicable, those responsible for their interpretation and appeasement had their work cut out.

Offerings, either buried or thrown into water, are the best sources of evidence about this most personal and revealing aspect of any society. Understandably the precarious nature of what was predominantly a subsistence economy geared fundamentally to the production of enough food led to a spiritual acknowledgement of the centrality of the agricultural cycle in everyone's lives. Animals, crops and the technology associated with them were all used as offerings to deities that might intervene favourably in the future, though large caches of metalwork have also been found in the south and east. It's unfortunately not clear whether the whole community was involved in the solemn presentation of each important gift or whether this was yet another example of conspicuous consumption by a few key members. Whichever, these sacred ceremonies would certainly occupy an important place in the social calendar of each tribe, however

Bronze horse ornaments found in a moss at Middleby, Annandale, which may have been offerings.

The prehistoric religious site in Temple Woods, Kilmartin.

many of its individual members were actually allowed to take part. Special places – in woods, bogs, rivers, lochs and even caves – gave added significance to the whole process.

With the abandonment of the great Neolithic burial sites, it is presumed that most people were now cremated, which doesn't mean that the whole process of saying goodbye to the dead was any less elaborate or important. By the end of this period, burial in disused buildings was also practised, though excarnation beforehand was probably still customary. The peoples of this society were not squeamish about using various bits and pieces of the dead in elaborate rituals and totems in and around domestic buildings, as well as sacred places. Whatever was deemed likely to bring good luck to the household and community formed part of the rich spiritual life of this period. Human sacrifice was not a commonplace event, but it did take place, presumably in times of extreme danger when extraordinary measures needed to be taken.

By the end of the Iron Age, a quite different society from the Mesolithic/early Neolithic had now evolved – definitely settled, with a wide range of contacts, possibly more hierarchical in some places, and with definite identities applying over increasingly larger areas. The metals that gave the more dominant groups both the instruments and the symbols of increased power had evolved with society and iron would continue to be adapted as a weapon of war for thousands more years.

It is not at all clear whether society's leaders were warriors and priests combined, or whether the two sides of the power coin operated in a mutually sustaining relationship. It is unfortunate that these later Prehistoric peoples seem to have lost interest in building durable tombs that might have provided some answers to these questions. On the other hand, impressive structures like the hillforts and crannogs designed for the living provide glimpses of high-powered gatherings for trade, ritual and, potentially, government.

It is not possible to know for certain if all these social and political changes caused more tension in general. But the fact that the population had reached the limits of the available land, pushing some people into undesirable areas, combined with a definite change in a range of environmental conditions, from the weather to the amount of peat, meant that the potential for conflict was becoming greater. On the other hand, the creation of larger power blocs beyond the local laid the foundations for the development of embryonic kingdoms. Such a development, which is a huge leap in social organization, was certainly not inevitable, nor predictable at this stage. But the process would certainly be pushed on by an overwhelming threat from outside.

FOUR

Amalgamation
AD 80 – 800

It is traditional to begin this period with the Romans, which is rather misleading, for the simple reason that most of what was about to become Scotland rarely encountered them and there is at least as much continuity with the Neolithic/Iron Age past as there is profound change. Nevertheless, for some reason many of us, whether at school or elsewhere, have been given the impression that the general pattern of history tracing the development of countries such as England and France which underwent the full Roman experience also applies to Scotland.

However, there are two good reasons for beginning this next phase with the arrival of the imperial armies. Firstly, it can't be denied that the Romans have provided the first written evidence for Scotland, though obviously such documents must be handled with care. Secondly, the attempted imposition of control from outside did ultimately promote a degree of unity among the otherwise fractious tribes and gave considerable impetus to the eventual creation of the embryonic state of Scotland itself.

Nevertheless, there is a tendency now to view the entire period up until the formation of Scotland after 800 AD as essentially one, so we should not forget the lessons from earlier prehistory. There was trade before the Romans arrived and after they left; styles of building and settlement continued to reflect the topography and climate of distinct areas;

A bronze cauldron discovered during the excavation of Roman remains in Peebles.

Memorial stone erected to mark the site of the Roman camp at Trimontium, near Melrose.

culture and identity were already developing and just because state structures had not emerged does not mean that the early peoples of Scotland were uncivilized.

Indeed, perhaps it could be argued that the most significant thing about the Roman Empire for Scotland was its demise. As the barbarian hordes (another one-sided view.) drove their way west across Europe, the institution which picked up the pieces of imperial civilization was not the state but the church. And the church was to continue to mould and shape the society at whose heart it lay throughout most of the middle ages. The migrations of peoples, too, had a profound effect on the history of Scotland, despite the fact that it lay at the western-most edge of Europe. So let us concentrate less on Roman armies, roads, trade, and especially baths, and spend more time on natives, invaders, monks and heroes.

At the time the Romans arrived in Scotland around 82 AD, over a century after Julius Caesar first landed on British soil, the existing tribes of Scotland were both numerous and distinct from one another. The Imperial legions under Agricola began to seriously make a play for the final portion of mainland Britain to add to their vast list of conquests in 79 AD, advancing across the Tyne and pushing up to the Forth-Clyde line. This first phase was accompanied, as was usual, by a flurry of fort-building activity. Only then would the advance legions feel that their backs were secure as they passed north of the Forth into the shadowy treacherous terrain that they called Caledonia. We are fortunate that they did so, since they have provided us with the first written opinions on the peoples living there.

The Romans doubtless expected the barbarian tribes of the north to behave in pretty much the same way as barbarian tribes of their vast domains usually did prior to conquest: put up an admirable, if futile, resistance, then succumb to both the might and the attractions of the rule of Rome. Descriptions of the battle fought perhaps in the shadow of Bennachie in Aberdeenshire against the Caledonians are revealing not just because their heroic leader, Calgacus, was given the honour of being the first-ever named 'Scot'. The long eulogy to freedom attributed to (or composed for) him by the Roman writer, Tacitus – including the immortal line, 'They create a desert and call it peace' – indicates the invaders' mixed feelings towards their own activities.

But those in the front line probably had little time to dwell on such niceties. They had far too much to do marching and building forts, as well as smoking the enemy out of numerous bogs and thickets. However, recent work suggests that Roman rumours of a wall-to-wall Great Wood of Caledon were hugely exaggerated in order to explain failure to military commanders elsewhere. As we have already seen, much of Scotland's wooded cover had already been cleared for settlement and what was left was likely be much more open than modern forests.

And anyway, the fate of the Romans in Scotland only depended on the counter-activities of the native tribes to a limited extent. Of far more importance was the troubled politics of the empire as it began to decline. Within a decade (86 AD) Agricola was forced to pull his men back out of the north to prop up front lines elsewhere. Forty years later, in 122, the unexpected persistence of this situation was acknowledged with the construction of Hadrian's Wall, the northernmost limit of Empire. Twenty years after this a second

A stone marking the grave of a Roman soldier, Glenalmond.

Inscribed Roman tablet from the Castlehill Station, Antonine Wall.

determined effort was made to bring the northern tribes into the fold, accompanied by the construction of the Antonine Wall even further north. But by the 160s everyone was safely back behind Hadrian's wall.

By this time either the Caledonian tribes were in the mood to give the Romans a taste of their own medicine or they were now well aware of the rich pickings to be had from those in the south who had adopted a Roman lifestyle. Whatever, the wall itself came under attack. By 208, it proved possible to initiate another set of campaigns – just as well, given that peace treaties and downright bribery were failing to work. As the century progressed the Empire began to disintegrate in earnest and by the end of it Britain as a whole was declaring its independence from Rome. Further campaigning did take place, even in the north, but a century later the Empire was on its last legs. In 410 Alaric the mighty Goth achieved the unthinkable – the taking of Rome. From now on there was a new set of forces at work in European politics, and a new set of invaders.

The native peoples of Scotland who faced the Romans were the direct descendants of the prehistoric tribes we have already met. But where they seem to have differed from their predecessors is in the extent to which they now accepted hierarchy and centralization in their societies. We cannot actually point to any clear-cut evidence for chiefs and lordly families generally living in top-of-the-range accommodation, hogging most of the disposable resources in taxes and having exquisite jewellery and other objects made to ensure that their status was quite obvious for all to see until at least a few centuries BC. This might have been happening in some places, but we shouldn't generalize.

The term 'Caledonians', according to the Romans, encompassed a multitude of tribes, of whom the most significant early on seem to have been the Maeatae. The Picts make their first appearance in 297, but even they were known to comprise separate groupings. By the mid-fourth century, the Picts (still a division of the Caledonians) were being subdivided into Verturions and Dicalydones. At the same time, we first hear of the Scots, a group operating in conjunction with the Picts but clearly *not* Caledonians. Whether or not the Romans fully understood the complex relationships among the northern tribes, this evidence suggests that these distinctive groups were now capable of working together in some kind of confederation, though the Picts were clearly becoming dominant, at least among the Caledonian tribes.

Having faced and effectively repelled one invader from the south, the native tribes of the north were soon to face another, more serious challenge. In the 470s southern England was finally reached by the Teutonic migrants displaced by the various peoples who had forced their way west from the Russian steppes over the previous centuries. The Anglo-Saxons had arrived in Britain. There was no immediate impact on the north; nevertheless, this event eventually had very serious repercussions once the Anglo-Saxon kingdom of Northumbria began to take shape immediately to the south of Pictland and the British kingdoms of the west of Scotland by the mid-sixth century.

The Picts

The Picts are probably the best-known but most enigmatic of the early Scottish peoples. Their art work and archaeological remains clearly indicate that theirs was no primitive society; yet they have left us almost nothing in writing to tell us directly about themselves.

It was once thought that the Picts spoke a different language of non-Indo-European origin but that has turned out not to be true. Though it is rather sad that we don't even know what they called themselves, it is certain that the Caledonian tribes all spoke a Celtic language, as did the Scots of the west and the Britons of the south-west. However, the Scots spoke a rather different version, called Q-Celtic which was more similar to Irish Gaelic, as opposed to the P-Celtic languages shared by the others.

The process of centralization, which tentatively began in the late Bronze Age, eventually gave the Pictish leaders the ability to control most of eastern and northern Scotland. Pictland was supposedly divided into seven provinces, corresponding, to some extent, with the earldoms that emerged after 1000 AD: Fortriu (Strathearn and Menteith); Fib (Fife); Fothriff (Kinross); Circinn (Angus and the Mearns); Fotla (Atholl); Catt (Caithness); Ce and Fidach (north of the river Dee).

The key difference between the Picts and their prehistoric ancestors is perhaps most starkly illustrated at Gurness on Orkney. We have already noted the existence of an imposing broch there, but at some point when it came to be situated in Pictland a village of squat inferior buildings was built round it. Now there was definitely a lord and master in residence in the broch with his family, while the rest lived outside.

Sea power was very important to the Picts and a large fleet was maintained, possibly at their great power centre at Burghead on the Moray coast. Much of the prime agricultural land in Scotland lay within their domains, so powerful networks were required to ensure that the grain and other agricultural produce paid in taxes was all accounted for. And thus the members of the Pictish nobility accumulated the wealth that enabled them to commission the craftsmen capable of producing the awesome

The 'Eaglestone' at Strathpeffer, one of the many beautifully carved megaliths crested by Pictish craftsmen.

An elaborate Pictish hunting scene carved on a stone sarcophaguc.

carved stones for which they are renowned, and to indulge in the activities depicted on the stones.

Hunting was now very much an aristocratic pursuit, as it had been for many centuries already. Men and women both took part in these essentially social occasions, which were doubtless used as opportunities to display their wealth and skill. The nobility, along with their leaders, lived apart from the hoi polloi in buildings which we can now confidently assert were designed to inspire awe and admiration. By the early medieval period (after 500 AD) these could take the form of a new type of hill-fort, such as Dundurn, carefully constructed to differentiate between social groups even within their walls, or of palaces, such as that at Fortriu, situated on the lower ground, often part of larger power complexes that might eventually include Christian sources of spiritual power.

Pictish kings were powerful men, though the fact that, as elsewhere, succession to the throne was open to many branches of the royal family meant that there was frequently a bloody competition for power. Political executions, often by drowning, were a definite feature of this society. The interrelationship between spiritual authority and earthly power continued and kings maintained wizards or shamans at their courts to impress on the population at large the continuing closeness of royal communion with the other world. Religion of this kind was not about personal redemption but collective survival in the form of official bargaining with the notoriously fickle elements.

The Picts traded with the other power groups within the British Isles (and beyond) and were happy to borrow cultural ideas when it suited them – many of the designs on the marvellous Pictish stones seem to have been Northumbrian in origin. All the main tribal groups that later amalgamated to form Scotland went to war with each other at various times during the first millennium AD. But that didn't prevent them from being close in other ways. Intermarriage was a product of war, being used as an integral feature of peace treaties until only a few centuries ago. The ensuing blood relationships among the elites of warring tribes led at the very least to a cultural cross-pollination, even if peace itself was far from guaranteed.

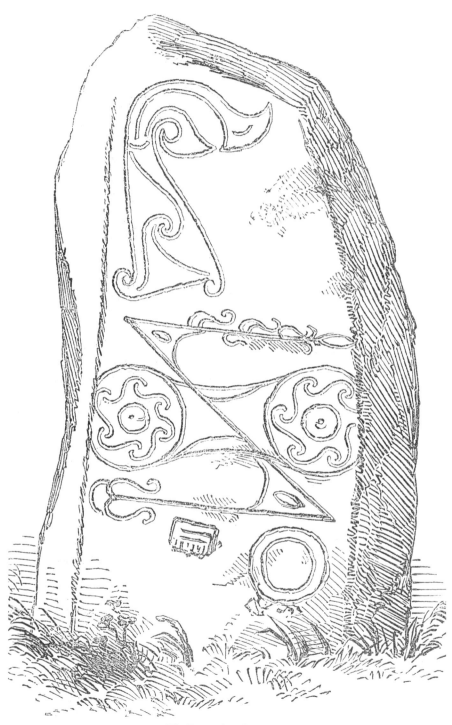

The Dunnichen Stone.

We should also remember that they naturally shared the same basic values anyway. As elites formed through their ability to protect and aggrandize the tribe, they enjoyed pastimes such as the hunt and the feast, as well as actually going to war, softened to some extent in the last centuries of the millennium by the teachings of the Church. It should therefore come as no real surprise to see the nobility throughout the British Isles demanding similar things of their craftsmen, builders, poets and, eventually, priests, even if the precise ways of expressing them might be different.

The Scots

The Scots, in this period, are more generally thought of as Irish, for the simple reason that the traditional story has them arriving from Ireland to settle in and around Argyll around 500 AD in order to join the Picts in their struggle against the Romans. The problem with this version of events, which turns up in Scottish chronicles written a few centuries later, is that it's hard for archaeologists to explain why, in that case, the material remains show so little direct connection with Ireland.

The traditional story relates that Fergus Mor mac Eirc, an Antrim prince, established his new kingdom in Argyll itself, Knapdale, Kintyre and Cowal. His descendants founded various families, or clans, the main ones being the Cenel nGabrain (originally the main branch of the extended royal family but not always the dominant one), the Cenel nOengusa and the Cenel Loairn. According to a remarkable document, the *Senchus Fer nAlban*, these clans could muster at least 1,500 men. Given the importance of sea power, the fighting unit was not a soldier for land battalions, but an oarsman for boats. Written several centuries before the Domesday Book, the *Senchus* is the earliest known post-Roman tax assessment in the British Isles.

Sure, the people of the Scottish kingdom of Dal Riata had very close relations with their nearest neighbours across the water, both politically and culturally – the similarity of the languages spoken on either side of the Irish Sea indicates that. It may even have been the case that a member of an Irish royal family inherited the leadership of Dal Riata in Scotland. But there was almost certainly no wholesale migration and the replacement of native peoples by a new wave of Celtic incomers. At a basic level, the prehistoric communities of the western seaboard remained intact, even if their leaders came from new stock. Indeed, such changes at the top began to occur with increasing regularity, thanks again to intermarriage, as these distinct but small kingdoms began to coalesce into the larger kingdom of Scotland.

The Scots did, of course, eventually give their name to that new political unit, which is surprising, when you think about it. The formidable mountainous barrier that cuts off Argyll and the west from the low-lying plains of central Scotland made the Irish sea world a far more obvious political playground for the inhabitants of Dal Riata. But the pressure placed on the Picts by the Anglo-Saxons led them to look west and those who had stood firm together against the Romans now became enemies. Ironically, this also ensured that Dal Riatan kings took part in eastern and southern politics when their more natural inclination may well have been to look predominantly west.

The Scottish **kings** of Dal Riata held sway over one of the most sophisticated political units of the period. From their pre-eminent seat of power at Dunadd – one of the new type of hill forts that we've already met in Pictland – set in the heart of a ritual landscape of ancient symbolic importance, they presided over a court which boasted the very best in European imports, the finest metalwork produced by craftsmen in residence, and a cosmopolitan mix of visitors. On the other hand, the prevalence of warfare, both campaigns against outside enemies and squabbles among the descendants of the early Dal Riatan kings, left even Dunadd occasionally vulnerable to attack and destruction.

> **A word about kingship**
>
> We tend to take it for granted that a king (and these days a queen) should succeed through *primogeniture*, ie. through the eldest son of a previous monarch (or the next eldest if he then had no children and then through the girls if absolutely necessary). But that could leave young children in charge, a most undesirable situation in a warrior society. *Tanistry*, where kings are chosen from among the adult males of the wider royal family, made far more sense. But such a system did lead to fights for the throne, like that most famously described in Shakespeare's *Macbeth*.

But what gave these Scottish kings even greater prestige was their association with a new source of power in the north: Christianity. With Columba's success in establishing a monastery on Iona (see below), the Scottish kings had easy access to a far more complex form of moral authority than the old magic. This religion explicitly addressed the issue of why some men were placed over others, binding king and priest together in a divinely sanctioned hierarchy.

The Scottish kings have left us the clearest evidence, in the form of the large footprint embedded in rock at Dunadd, of the symbolism associated with kingship (though I don't know what happened if your foot didn't fit!). Admittedly this ceremony had decidedly

Chess pieces from Uig on the Isle of Lewis, representing a king and queen enthroned.

animals often sharing the space. These distinctive and lofty buildings certainly look as if theywere the homes of important leaders and their families, and probably were. Some brochs, like that at Gurness on Orkney, now have the remains of villages surrounding them, but, as we shall see, these villages were built much later than the brochs.

In the centuries leading up to the birth of Christ, brochs seem to have been replaced by wheelhouses, another architectural type characteristic of these exposed coasts. These weren't as tall as the brochs, meaning that they weren't so impressive outside. But inside their builders have provided showpieces for their skills in drystane dyking, constructing a series of curved pillars parallel and partly attached to the circular outer wall and supporting the stone outer edge of the roof – hence the name, wheelhouse.

By the later Iron Age, it seems likely that distinctive power blocs based in Shetland and Caithness centred themselves on particular brochs, which may indeed have acted as homes to men best described as kings. Although they seem to date from slightly later, the wheelhouses perhaps came into use to distinguish important families from those both above and below them in the social order. And though we might regard these areas as isolated and remote today, the admittedly scarce evidence does seem to indicate surprisingly vibrant connections with other parts of Britain and Europe in terms of trade and diplomacy.

The people of these coastal areas faced particular problems with environmental change, as they became more exposed to colder, wetter weather and, more particularly, the **advance of peat**. They could still farm crops, but animals, both husbanded and hunted, were at least as important to their economy. In more temperate areas, however, the evidence for field systems suggests that the growing of crops was the main farming activity and pushed to the limits of capacity.

The evidence of souterrains – underground passages attached to houses – may back this up. Though the jury is still out on exactly what role they played in the Iron Age economy, the theory that they might have been used for storage would imply a huge surplus of foodstuffs being generated in the south and east particularly. The fact that souterrains were found all over these areas and were attached to ordinary houses also implies that the community as a whole, rather than just an elite, still controlled this surplus.

Increasingly complex interiors, providing smaller, more private, spaces, suggest that particular members of the family now had their own space, though the hearth tended to act as the focal point. But beyond these basics, we're still not sure how exactly people organized themselves. Roman writers suggest that polygamy was practised but we should not automatically believe them since the native peoples of Scotland were, after all, enemies of Rome and basically portrayed as painted savages, a view that is, to put it charitably, extremely prejudiced.

The advance of peat

Peat advances for four main reasons - changes in the soil, climate decline, burning and tree clearance. It seems to have begun c.7600 BC, but it is very difficult to plot its expansion, and explain why it did so.

We know so much more about how Iron Age people lived simply because the evidence is much thicker on the ground. And one of the main reasons for that is the growing tendency to use stone instead of wood, perhaps as a response to more unpleasant and 6000 individuals. But given these hill forts' exposure to the elements and distance from the arable fields which presumably fed their inhabitants, it has been suggested that these were not permanently settled but acted as important focal points, as seats of government, or for special ceremonies or trading extravaganzas at particular times. The walls were probably there, then, primarily for show, not defence, though they could presumably be used for that if necessary.

In the northern and western coastal areas, the most distinctive form of architecture emerging in this period was the brochs, though they were descendants of earlier roundhouses. Again, given the resources needed to build such structures, this may be evidence of increased centralization, although, unlike some of the hill settlements, brochs can't actually accommodate that many people (perhaps around thirty). Despite the high walls, the primary living areas seem to have been confined to the ground or first floor, with

An imposing broch tower on the isle of Lismore.

A broch at Glenelg.

The Ruthwell Cross illustrates the fusion of Christian symbolism with native Scottish aesthetics.

pagan aspects to it, the footprint perhaps symbolizing the marriage of king and land. But the Christian element was associated with a rather controversial element of the relationship between king and priest. Did the role of the priest in a royal inauguration imply that he actually created the king (it was later alleged that Columba himself performed such a ceremony for the Dal Riatan king) or was there really no earthly person between the monarch and god? Such questions were to cause increasingly bitter arguments for over a thousand years.

There was nothing inevitable about the eventual absorption of the Pictish kingship by the Dal Riatan royal family and the subsequent creation of the new larger kingdom of Alba/Scotland after 800 (see below and Chapter Five). But there can be no doubt that, once it had happened, these Scottish kings and their advisers were quite capable of making it look all very well worked out. That did mean tampering a little bit with what was known of the past, to incorporate the Pictish monarchs into the Scottish king lists and develop the story of a pure line of Celtic people who had come over from Ireland to Scotland.

That story soon became very necessary as the developing Anglo-Saxon kingdom of England began to construct another story which stated that Britain had been divided among a royal brood of sons, the eldest of which, Brutus, received England as his share.

It didn't take long for it to be stated explicitly that this therefore meant that the rulers of other parts of the British isles were not just inferior but subject to the kings of England.

The Britons

Like the Picts, the British tribes of the south-west experienced a long period of consolidation before they could be described as belonging to the kingdom of Strathclyde. By that time, they had endured considerable pressure from the south and east as the Anglo-Saxons sought to extend their territory. Where once the Britons had formed a loose confederation that extended south from the Clyde all the way to Cornwall, the northern end of the chain had become isolated from the rest by the middle of the millennium, thanks to Anglo-Saxon expansion. The centre of this truncated British kingdom lay at Alt Clun – mighty Dumbarton rock – which controlled the sea entry to western Scotland at the highest navigable point on the Clyde. Sea travel must also have been vital to the maintenance of the power of the British kings, linking them into a western network which included the Scottish kingdom to the north, as well as Ireland and the western seaboard of England.

The Britons could claim an even longer link with Christianity than the Scots, since the first known mission to Scotland was undertaken in the south-west by Ninian, who set up an ecclesiastical centre at Whithorn, though it's doubtful whether Christianity actually took root as early as that. When it did, the main official centre of Christianity in Strathclyde became Govan on the Clyde. There, and elsewhere, we can see the remains – carved stones, crosses and sarcophagi – of a vibrant warrior society whose spirituality was

St Ninian's Church on the isle of Whithorn, arguably the first major Christian site in Scotland.

Left: Sixth-century boundary stone from Whithorn. The inscription reads: 'The place of St Peter the Apostle'. Above: A collection of ancient artefacts, Whithorn Priory Museum.

fervent and beautifully expressed. The Britons, like the Picts, were also quite happy to borrow from Anglo-Saxon culture; if such art and poetry was regarded as the best around, then they were quite happy to use it.

The British royal family also took part in the intermarriage merry-go-round that was part and parcel of the apparently endless bouts of warfare among the four nations. As a result, they too were related to the other royal houses and were ultimately absorbed into Alba (the embryonic kingdom of Scotland – see below and Chapter Five) when an Alban king became a king of Strathclyde too. But before then, the Britons of Strathclyde had been a distinct and powerful people, playing their own part in the wider politics of this island. This distinctiveness continued long after there was no longer a separate kingdom, finding expression in laws and customs particular to the south-west and the enduring independent tendencies of Galloway in particular.

The Anglo-Saxons

As already mentioned, the Anglo-Saxons were the new tribe on the block in the fifth century but they didn't take long to emerge as a force to be reckoned with throughout the British Isles. Within only a few generations of their arrival from the Continent, they had pushed the British tribes of England further and further west and set up their own mini-kingdoms across the east and centre of the country (not that England existed at that time any more than Scotland did). From Scotland's point of view, the main source of trouble came from the two Anglo-Saxon kingdoms immediately to the south, Deira and Bernicia.

In the first few decades of the seventh century, the threat from the south became even more powerful when these two kingdoms amalgamated into one, forming Northumbria. But even before then, the Anglo-Saxons had fixed their attention on the land immediately to the north, the territory of the British tribe the Votadini, centred on what became Edinburgh. Despite the heroic imagery created in the poetry of the Gododdin, they were no match for their southern neighbours, meeting spectacular defeat at Catraeth (usually associated with the modern Catterick Bridge) in the mid- to late sixth century. But it was the battle of Degestan in 603 that sealed the fate of southern Scotland. The Dal Riatan king, Aidan, and possibly the Britons of Strathclyde, were unable to stem the tide of Anglo-Saxon success and the Northumbrian kingdom could now claim to wield authority as far as the Forth. Next stop: Pictland. However, despite their many successes, they were not invincible, as we shall see.

Given their close links with the Continent from which they had so recently migrated, the Anglo-Saxons, once they had accepted Christianity about 627, were keen to link in with the southern, Roman version of it and, through it, to a wider European society. Though these were clearly a warrior people, they also seem to have seen little contradiction in the relationship between war and religion (though their priests probably did). The poetry and art sponsored by them was profound, beautiful and highly influential.

It is not surprising, also, that they should have brought with them many aspects of Continental life, including building styles. One of the most obvious examples of Anglo-Saxon architecture was the great timber halls (sometimes also built in stone), which played host to the extravagant feasts that were part and parcel of the warrior lifestyle. By the end of the seventh century, many of the trappings of the Roman 'good life', including glass, were available again in the Anglo-Saxon kingdoms. In Scotland the predilection was still to use timber and heather or reeds for their buildings.

The Anglo-Saxons were also fortunate in producing one of the earliest historians of these islands – the Venerable Bede. His *Ecclesiastical History of the English People*, which stands out as one of the earliest descriptions of life in Britain in the eighth century, has perhaps been relied on more than it should simply because there is so little else with which to compare it. Bede had very definite opinions about some of the other peoples occupying the British Isles – he was generally none too flattering about the Picts and the Scots, for example – and we should be cautious about relying on him too much.

The amalgamation of the Anglo-Saxon kingdoms into England, traditionally credited to Alfred of Wessex and his cakes, is not of direct relevance to this story, though relations between the developing kingdoms of Scotland and England will certainly feature. But it should be clear that the Anglo-Saxons did play an important role in the development of Scotland, not least because Lothian and the Borders spent nearly 500 years, up until 1018, as part of Northumbria.

The Church

The establishment of Christianity in Scotland was a major political, economic and social, as well as spiritual, development. Admittedly it didn't happen overnight – on more than one occasion a campaign of conversion was followed by a relapse to familiar pagan ways, and we should also recognize the extent to which the old traditions were often amalgamated into the new belief system, to make it more acceptable.

The first major attempt at conversion began with Ninian, a Briton with Roman connections, in the south-west. But the man credited with being the father of Christianity in Scotland was, of course, Columba. We may never know exactly why he chose (or was forced) to leave his native Ireland for the more remote parts of the western seaboard. We don't even know which king – Pictish or Scottish – granted him the island of Iona to set up a new monastery.

But it would be churlish to deny the huge influence which this sixth-century monk had on Scottish history in general and the development of the Scottish church in particular. And this despite the fact that, contrary to general belief, he seems to have ventured off Iona on a conversion mission on only one verifiable occasion, into the heart of Pictland. And he doesn't even seem actually to have succeeded in converting either King Bridei or the Picts. The secret of his long-term success? A glowing

A fascinating example of the fusion of Christianity and native Scottish legend is 'Queen Vanora's Stone' at Meigle. On the one side, a beautiful Celtic cross, on the other, the distinctly pagan story of Queen Vanora (possibly connected with the Wanor, or Guinevere, of Arthurian legend) being torn to pieces by furious animals.

Kirk Michael Cross, Isle of Man. Ancient Scotland, especially Dal Riata, formed part of a wider Irish Sea cultural and religious community along with Man and of course Ireland.

biography written by Adomnan, one of his successors as abbot of Iona around 700.

Columba, or at least Adomnan, recognized that churchmen, even those dedicated to the contemplative life, should act as the mouthpiece of God's word and try to influence kings to behave in a more Christian fashion. However, in the centuries after Columba, the Church in Britain and Ireland also spent quite a bit of time arguing within itself about specific details of clerical and doctrinal behaviour. The increasing influence of Rome as the western centre of Christianity meant that Iona lost its pre-eminent position to the monastery at Lindisfarne, which had subscribed to the Roman view for longer, despite having begun as an offshoot of Iona. However, Columba's monastery continued to be a major centre of pilgrimage and learning.

The strong association of the Columban church with the Scots of Dal Riata in particular ensured that the saint and his monastery would become fundamental to the development of Scotland itself. The growing need to thrash out a history entirely separate from the Anglo-Saxon kingdom of England ensured that the Scottish church became a major force in the development of a distinctive Scottish identity and soon pushed that identity down a defiantly Irish route.

And, as the sole practitioners of a new and very powerful magic – the ability to read and write – churchmen became indispensable to kings as the latter expanded their administrations and paid more attention to the impression their developing kingdoms were making on the outside world. Let us not forget one essential fact: everything we know about medieval Scotland, whether from government documents or chronicles, was written by a churchman, and many were actually composed by them. Whether they were engaged in high politics, education or farming, these men were a dynamic force in Scotland's history.

Bringing Scotland together

Alba – the Gaelic word for Britain – was used initially to describe the kingdom that emerged after 800 AD from the acquisition of the Pictish kingship by the Dal Riatan kings. (Ironically, Dal Riata itself was not included within Alba's boundaries, predominantly because it was dealing with a new invader – see Chapter Five.) But the creation of a new kingdom comprising much of Pictland but ruled by Scottish kings was perhaps one of the more unlikely scenarios, given the history of the previous centuries. For much of that time, it might have seemed more likely that most of what became Scotland would be absorbed into the expanding Anglo-Saxon kingdom of Northumbria.

Having reached the Forth at the beginning of the seventh century, the Anglian kings had no intention of stopping there. To begin with they contented themselves with seeing a succession of puppet kings installed in Pictland. The later seventh century saw them reach the height of their power, with much of Pictland actually taken into Northumbria and tribute exacted even from parts of Dal Riata. Ecgfrith of Northumbria decided to go the whole hog in 671, perhaps because his puppet Pictish king had been ousted, and yet again an Anglo-Saxon army triumphed. Dal Riata was also in disarray, plagued by constant fighting among the kingdom's most powerful families, a civil war that prompted the earliest recorded sea battle in British history in 719.

But then the Anglo-Saxons stopped having things all their own way. The Picts were the first

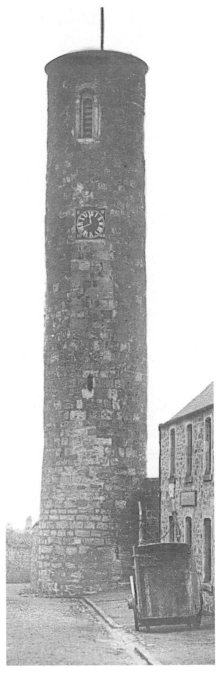

The Round Tower, Abernethy. According to Bede the building of the stone church here – of which the tower is all that remains – was ordered by the Pictish king Nechtan in AD 711.

to recover their assertiveness. Their king, another Bridei, who was actually a Briton and closely related to the royal family of Strathclyde, defeated and killed Ecgfrith at the battle of Nechtansmere near Forfar in 685. This may be the military event depicted on the nearby Aberlemno Stone, though it was actually carved at least a century later. Bridei dealt not only with the Anglian threat but did much to restore active royal authority throughout most of Pictland.

Pictland was also fortunate in having a succession of dynamic and successful kings to follow Bridei. By the middle of the eighth century Angus mac Fergus had not only managed to ensure Pictland's independence but had actually captured Dunadd and established himself as overlord of Dal Riata. He then turned his attention on the British kingdom of Strathclyde, ironically using the Northumbrians as allies. Had Angus had been successful, which he wasn't, the Picts might well have become the dominant nation within an embryonic larger country (we can't call it Scotland, of course – it was given that name because the Scots were the dominant people).

But Angus died in 761 and the tide turned against the Picts. Within twenty years Dal Riata had re-emerged as an autonomous kingdom ready to turn the tables on its eastern neighbours. Pictland began to show signs of disintegration as the lands of the far north returned to the semi-autonomous state that they had probably enjoyed before Bridei knocked them back into submission. Then, in 789 a member of one of the leading Dal Riatan families (Cenel nGabhrain) managed to take over the leadership of both the Scottish kingdom and Pictland.

At that point only an extremely imprudent gambler would have placed money on Dal Riata having succeeded in taking over Pictland on a more permanent basis. The dynastic changes that took place with alarming regularity at the head of all these nations made that extremely unlikely, although, interestingly, a son had succeeded his father as king in Pictland only a few years earlier.

Ironically, one of the reasons why Alba began to emerge as a coherent entity was because much of northern Scotland and the western seaboard was now being devastated by one of the most formidable European warrior nations, the Vikings. For those experiencing the destruction at first hand, the emergence of a new vigorous kingdom was the last thing they might have imagined. But the seeds had been sown.

FIVE

Consolidation and Assimilation
800 – 1286

The birth of Alba was a long, drawn-out and certainly far from inevitable development, although the process of consolidation, sometimes but not always into embryonic kingdoms, was happening elsewhere too. Most of the peoples that eventually could be said to live in Scotland – Picts, Scots, Britons and Anglo-Saxons – had made each other's acquaintance in both peace and war over hundreds of years. There had been considerable opportunities for genuine familiarity – through intermarriage, trade and cultural exchange, and membership of the universal Christian church. So, despite the blood and thunder associated with the warlike ventures on which they seem to have spent much of their time, their coming together in one nation was not quite as daft as might initially be supposed. This slow process was possibly also very similar to earlier amalgamations of smaller groups long before the idea of a nation was thought of. However, there was a long way to go yet, and not all possible avenues of development led to Scotland.

In the mid-790s the Viking longships moved boldly round the northern coast of Scotland towards the western Isles. The main impetus behind this terrifying exodus was a basic shortage of land back home in Scandinavia. There was no lack of actual land mass but much of it plunges almost vertically into the sea – there just wasn't the room to expand farming capacity at a time of increasing population.

The Vikings have endured fairly consistent depictions of their cruelty and destruction throughout history, though more recently attempts have been made to rehabilitate them as farmers and settlers. The consensus these days seems to be that they were probably both.

In the initial stages, when the pressure on land was not so overwhelming, the impetus to go abroad was perhaps restricted to the younger men who had nothing to lose, and glory, not to mention quick riches, to gain. Later on, as the population back home continued to rise, the need to find somewhere else to live on a permanent basis prompted a more usual form of emigration, presumably including women and children. Viking seamanship and sense of adventure are still spectacular by anyone's standards: they established themselves in places as far apart as North America, Greenland, Normandy (Norman = Northman), Sicily and Russia, as well as huge swathes of the British Isles.

But for those whom they first encountered, the experience was just plain ugly: murder, large-scale looting and general mayhem were the usual results of a short, sharp Viking raid. Iona was attacked first in 795, though it wasn't until 802 that it was sacked properly. Five years later, with many monks dead, the terrified survivors packed their bags and began to remove themselves to their sister monastery at Kells in Ireland. To the now fully Christian inhabitants of Scotland, the Vikings were damned not just through their violent actions, but by their paganism.

However, they did contribute greatly to the story of Scotland. In the first instance, their wider impact was political. The Dal Riatan dynasty which had taken over the Pictish kingship also found itself under Viking attack. Based at Fortriu in Perthshire, these kings proved no match for their aggressors and so failed in a primary element of their job description – to protect their people. The dynasty was overthrown. However, the real winner of this Viking intervention was Cinaed mac Alpin – Kenneth MacAlpin – who became king of the Scots and the Picts around 843.

However, as the Vikings began to settle, much of northern Scotland and the western seaboard quickly proved to be out of bounds to the burgeoning authority of the kings of Alba. This laid the groundwork in the west particularly for a quite different historical evolution that affected relations with the Scottish government well beyond the early middle ages.

By then, the Vikings could already be viewed as a force in Scottish and Irish politics, as opposed to a terrifying, but temporary, nuisance. They too joined the merry-go-round of political/military alliances which the Picts, Scots, Britons and Anglo-Saxons had engaged in for centuries, bringing in the Isle of Man and Ireland thanks to their western territorial influence.

Northumbria was still an important element in Scottish and English politics, but the emergence of a Wessex-dominated kingdom of England, combined with devastating Viking attacks down the east coast, had weakened it considerably. This was good news for the emerging kingdom of Alba, which began to encroach on territory south of the Forth. This culminated in the official relinquishing of Lothian by Northumbria to Alba in 973, though the English required a final reminder of this, duly administered at the battle of Carham in 1018.

A carved stone from Invergowrie showing unmistakeable Scandinavian-style craftsmanship.

Unfortunately, the weakening of Northumbria made it a target for the powerful Wessex kings, who then threatened Alba, at least to keep the northern kingdom out of the north of England. This came to a head in 937, when Athelstan, king of Wessex and York, inflicted a crushing military defeat on Constantine of Alba at Brunanburh near the Humber. The border between England and Scotland in the east was starting to take shape, though it took an extraordinarily long time for the kings of Scots to give up on pushing it further south. In the meantime, they concentrated on expanding to the west.

The British kingdom of Strathclyde was certainly not immune from either Viking attack or continuing encroachment from elsewhere. In some ways they had the worst set of neighbours, since they were completely encircled by competing powers, including the Norse king of Dublin. In 870 the latter, Olaf, managed to capture Dumbarton Rock, perhaps with Alban connivance, and married off his daughter to the leader of the Norse Hebrides, a mighty alliance indeed.

But yet again all this military activity had cultural and social spin-offs. The Gaels of the western seaboard who remained outside Alba had no choice but to live with the

Norse invaders but soon they became indistinguishable from each other. Interestingly, too, Gaelic survived as the dominant language, suggesting that the native population absorbed the Vikings, rather than the other way round, even where political leadership was Norse.

With the establishment of Norse kings in the west and a Norse earldom in Orkney (*c*.880), the same processes as we've already seen taking place before 800 – intermarriage, cultural intermixing – now extended to include them: at least one king of Alba boasted a Norse name, for example. The biggest barrier to greater assimilation was surely the fact that the Vikings preferred their own colourful pagan beliefs to Christianity until well into the eleventh century. But once they had joined the Christian community of Western Europe, they became full members of that larger cultural world. The distinctive hogback sarcophagus, perhaps representing a roof or even an upturned boat, was one of their particular contributions to religious expression. Examples of these can still be seen in Govan church, near Glasgow.

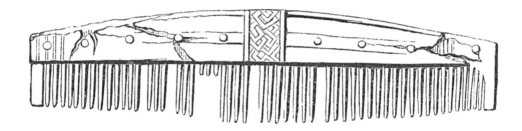

A comb (above) and brooch (below) from Pier-o-Whaal, Orkney. In the north and west of Scotland, resident Celts and settling Vikings achieved a seamless amalgamation of cultures.

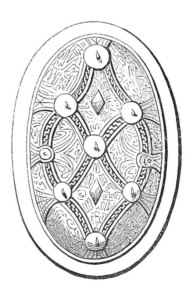

The weakness of Northumbria and Strathclyde at this point in time certainly made it easier for Alba to strengthen itself internally and then begin to expand its territory. But that, too, was no easy task: Alba, like Pictland before it, struggled with a political divide that coincided with the physical barrier of the Grampian mountains. Macbeth, in the eleventh century, would break the mould in taking the Scottish throne from his power base in Moray, north of the Mounth, as the physical divide was generally called. The dominant Alban royal families tended to be based in the south. The uncertainty of these times continued the desirability of maintaining a pool of adult male candidates for the throne, thus perpetuating the likelihood of fights over the kingship – a dynastic Catch-22.

But consolidation continued, despite military distractions. Perhaps an indication of this, so far as Alba is concerned, is the abandonment of the distinctive early medieval royal fortresses such as Dunadd and Dundurn, which seem to have outlived their usefulness by the ninth century. Their locations reflected the strategic priorities of an earlier age, though their status-oriented interiors were doubtless still useful. Most of the types of residence that we've already encountered continued to function – hillforts, crannogs, low-lying palace complexes, and, presumably (there is nothing much left to indicate them), the low-grade, timber-built houses that most people lived in.

Though we tend to pin the creation of Alba to either the reigns of Kenneth MacAlpin or the Fortriu kings of Pictland and Dal Riata, those living in Scotland at the time were certainly not aware that they were living in the embryonic Scottish state. However, around 900, we have the first explicit references to *Alba,* used for the first time to denote this new political entity and indicating a conscious effort to ignore the Pictish past. Contemporaries clearly did feel therefore that a significant change had taken place.

On the other hand, we must remember that those who used the term – the elites of both church and state – were also those who had most to gain from encouraging loyalty to Alba. Its use does not necessarily indicate that most Scots felt that very much had changed and many, such as those independent-minded folk north of the Mounth, were downright resistant to the new idea. Equally importantly, this was not Scotland as we know it today in terms of its geographical identity – considerable expansion, south, west and north, had to take place before the map was complete, and the exact dimensions were not predestined.

The church played a crucial role in the development of Alba. Its interests in promoting a strong kingdom were served in a number of ways, many of them perfectly laudable. Unity under a consolidated kingship would hopefully serve to lessen the constant violent rivalries that had certainly been a feature of previous centuries. Stability also encouraged economic development, something the church was very keen to be involved in.

As the kings' right-hand men – their administrators and propagandists – Scotland's leading churchmen played their role both internally, maintaining the mechanisms of government along with the nobles, and externally, representing the country in a range of international contexts. Their first loyalty supposedly lay with the pope in Rome, whose power and influence was increasing dramatically around 1000. But in reality the interests of church and state often coincided beautifully.

Above left: The handbell of St Columba, one of Scotland's most highly prized religious relics. These portable bells were venerated in the early medieval church and were often used for the swearing of oaths or the pronouncement of curses.

Above: The Kilmichael-Glassrie bell. Within the ornate brass shrine is a heavily corroded iron bell similar to that of St Columba.

Left: The Dunvegan Cup. This wooden chalice dates from the tenth century and bears the inscription: 'Ufo, son of John, son of Magnus, Prince of the Isle of Man, the grandson of Liahia Macgryneil, trusts in the Lord Jesus that mercy will be given to him in that day. Oneil Oimi made this in the year of our Lord 993.'

The monastery of Iona, though it suffered greatly at the hands of the Vikings, did not shut down completely. The Book of Kells, which most now agree probably came from Iona, was written around the turn of the second millennium and indicates the kind of high quality, Christian-orientated purchase which the higher nobility liked to have kicking around the castle. Given the key role that Columba and Iona played in Dal Riata, it's not too surprising that this should have continued beyond the take-over of Pictland and the creation of Alba. Many Scottish kings continued to be buried at the monastery until the end of the eleventh century and Columba remained *the* Scottish saint, until eventually subordinated by the exotic continental saint, Andrew.

Andrew, unlike Columba, never saw Scotland when he was alive, but his bones supposedly arrived there in the eighth century. Having the relics of a a bona fide apostle was a great coup. Indeed, the relics associated with both saints were an integral part of Scottish spiritual life, as well as totems of the nation's identity and well-being. But when one compares the huge and ornate sarcophagus which may have been constructed to hold Andrew's bones with the very lovely but decidedly portable *brecbennach* of Columba, it is not difficult to imagine rather different royal aspirations being invested in the saintly pair.

The shift of power to the east, which the take-over of Pictland and Viking activity had prompted, had repercussions for the Scottish church. Though Iona still functioned, its position was precarious. New, less vulnerable religious centres sprang up closer to the heartland of political power in east central Scotland, the main two being Dunkeld and Kinrymont/St Andrews. These centres often became bishoprics, their holders playing a key role in both the ecclesiastical and the state hierarchy, as overseers of the behaviour of the Christian faithful and senior administrators. The Culdee church – from *Céli Dé*, servants of God – was a highly organized spiritual powerhouse with its feet firmly in this world, however much it was busy preparing Scottish souls for the next.

The cross of Lauchlan McFingan, father of Abbot John of Iona (d. 1500). By this time Iona, though it had earned an unassailable place in the history of the Scottish church, had been eclipsed as an actual power centre by religious sites further east.

Above: An early seal of Holyrood Abbey, first noted on a charter of 1141 but with a style of workmanship that suggests an earlier date. The picture may represent the earliest timber buildings at Holyrood.

Left: The Pends, St Andrews.

Below: St Andrews Cathedral.

Secular power was also becoming highly organized. Kings and nobility, who had clearly devoted much of their energies in the middle part of the first millennium to an overt indulgence in, and celebration of, the cult of the warrior, were now refining their roles. The nobles were also the kings' right-hand men, usually on a much closer and more personal basis than their ecclesiastical counterparts. They still owed their positions to their abilities in war, but the lands and offices that they held gave their sons a head start in joining the inner circle. So, though nobility was technically not yet inherited explicitly 'by blood', and there was certainly scope for a man of talent and dynamism to rise through the ranks, the top layers of society were beginning to crystallize.

The basic system of administration, which sustained both individual noble estates and the kingdom itself, revolved, understandably, round the ability of the nation to feed itself. Taxation, collectable throughout the country, encompassed both the provision of actual foodstuffs and general hospitality. Hard cash was still regarded as an unnecessary form of taxation (after all, you can't eat it) and Scotland still didn't mint its own coinage. The lower orders stayed put, working to produce enough for themselves and their superiors; the elites moved about, attending to their administrative duties (not to mention leisure activities) and distributing the burden of their presence over a wide area.

The Scots, like their English contemporaries, had evolved their own system of government and administration long before the Normans arrived in England to redefine practices there. In Scotland, the key secular officers were the *mormaers*, who held regional power and were probably the descendants of earlier petty kings; and the *thanes*.

Mormaers, who later still often transformed themselves into earls, had the primary responsibility for organizing their locality for war, as well as forming the king's closest

Scotland's uncentralized power structure depended on a network of regional leaders, wielding power from small castles like this one at Little Cumbrae.

Kiesmuil Castle is one of three in Castle Bay, Barra. The geographically distant lords of the Western Isles had a great deal of freedom from the Scots crown.

circle of friends and advisers. They perhaps did not always relish their obvious subordinate role in the new Scotland and those furthest away from royal power in particular could often get away with acting as if they were still effectively independent. So long as power struggles for the throne remained a common occurrence, the opportunities for political advantage through supporting one candidate against another remained tempting, though the consequences of failure could be disastrous. Nevertheless, the increasing stability within the royal line by the beginning of the twelfth century meant that the rewards for independent action began to pale before the advantages of loyal royal service.

The thanes were the backbone of royal and noble administration, with the main responsibility for tax collection. These, too, were important men, living in demonstrably important buildings with a lifestyle to match. Despite the apparent simplicity of the terminology of status used above, the situation was far more complex – as perhaps it always has been. In particular, we should not forget that there was such a thing as the 'middling sort' long before the middle classes came into being. These men were usually substantial farmers who had an important voice to wield within the local community, even if they had little to say on the national stage. Given that so much administration, and therefore authority, remained rooted at a local level in Scotland, in contrast to England where it became extraordinarily centralized, the concentric circles of power which we can trace at the centre were replicated throughout society and were at least as important.

The infamous story of Macbeth, Duncan and Malcolm (not to mention Macduff), while saying much more about Shakespeare's early seventeenth-century world, illustrates

'…why upon this blasted heath you stop our way with such prophetic greeting': a picture postcard of the 'blasted heath' near Nairn. Macbeth's connection with the lands north of the Grampians may have contributed to his overthrow in 1057 and certainly made him an unusual king of Alba.

many of the above themes. Macbeth, and his wife, Gruoch, as members of the royal family, had reason to believe that they would succeed to the Scottish throne on the death of King Malcolm in 1034. However, Duncan, Malcolm's daughter's son, rather unusually became king (using descendants through a female line was usually avoided unless there was no alternative). This was not necessarily a popular choice, a factor compounded by proven military incompetence after he became king. Macbeth's claims, as well as his independence as ruler of Moray, prompted Duncan to take an army north in 1040, but the king was defeated in battle and his rival took his crown. As already mentioned, this shifted political power away from its Perthshire/southern heartland to the north, not least because of the support of Earl Torfinn of Orkney in helping Macbeth to the throne.

Nevertheless, Macbeth's seventeen-year reign was certainly not unsuccessful by the standards of the time, though he did have his problems, particularly through his relationship with the powerful Orcadian earl. His eventual downfall in 1057 at the hands of Malcolm, Duncan's son, was only accomplished with the help of Earl Sigurd of Northumberland. The role played by Macduff in Shakespeare's version may also reflect the anxieties of powerful lowland Scottish nobles reacting against the threat to their interests which the power shift to the north may have represented, a major dynamic in politics across time and place. *Plus ça change*.

However, Malcolm's seizure of the throne marked both an end and a beginning in Scottish politics. Thanks to the new king's own successful reign and the clutter of sons that he produced to follow him, 1057 began to draw a line under the dynastic infighting that had plagued kingship before that date. There were certainly challenges to the MacMalcolm dynasty, by descendants of former kings such as the MacWilliams and MacHeths, but they were beginning to be presented, by the central government at least, as the defiance of rebellious subjects on the periphery of political life, rather than traditional royal infighting. However, even though it had been quite usual to involve the Northumbrians in wars against rival kingdoms in previous centuries, the participation of a powerful English noble in Malcolm's rise to power proved to be a very mixed blessing indeed.

English influence on Scotland is a constant, and justifiable, theme in Scottish history, so long as such influence is treated in context and not viewed as the only defining element in the development of the northern kingdom. One of the most significant and controversial aspects of the interrelationship between the two countries is surely the arrival and subsequent pervasion (as opposed to invasion) of the Normans in Scotland and the introduction of the use of the F-word – feudalism.

There is nothing wrong with the term 'feudalism', if it is properly used. However, it does seem to have become something of a shorthand for a number of misleading and unhelpful mental images. It is certainly true for both Scotland and England that much of the apparent innovation in government and social/military organization often ascribed to the Normans owes more to their undoubted habit of writing just about everything down.

Scotland already had an effective system of administration. Many of the 'new' administrative/ecclesiastical units which seem to have taken root in the century or so after 1066 – sheriffdoms and bishoprics, for example – were almost certainly based on older ones. The king surely met with his key advisers whenever an affair of state required a consultation in the time before Norman influence inspired him to call it a parliament. We

William sails to England, from the Bayeux Tapestry. The conquest of Anglo-Saxon England by the Norman duke heralded a new era for the British Isles.

William sitting in state. With his army of clerics, William certainly possessed a great deal of written information about his new realm, but it is now being questioned whether this was linked to any great consolidation of royal authority.

should also note that the key parliamentary activity in England – getting an agreement on taxation – was largely unnecessary until much later in Scotland, simply because regular mass mobilization for war, which often triggered the need for taxes, was a very rare occurence.

Feudalism had its primary *raison d'être* in the calling out of an army and the holding of land, two sides of the same coin. In Scotland raising cavalry was done through the feudal model of grants of land for 40 days' annual military service. On the other hand, the old Celtic system of recruiting footsoldiers, instigated for centuries by the mormaers/earls from among the able-bodied in each region, remained the basic method. The fact that the cavalry in particular tended to be neither very effective nor very numerous only illustrates the essential point that in the first few centuries after 1000, utilizing Scotland's manpower in a military capacity gradually began to diminish in importance.

And yet the period after the accession of Malcolm III (from 1057) did witness extraordinary developments in many aspects of social and political life. Or maybe it only seems extraordinary because historians finally have the beginnings of a stream of documents with which they can work. Whichever, we now have a far clearer understanding of how Scottish government and administration, both secular and religious, worked at most levels.

For the vast majority of Scots, life would not have been transformed in any fundamental way. The greatest change, so far as arable farmers were concerned, had taken place around the ninth century with the introduction of the mouldboard plough, which allowed much heavier soils to be cultivated and turned over, producing deep ridges. Settlements, as ever, did not follow one pattern, but often fell into two basic types: tiny but clustered hamlets, associated with arable farming and therefore, generally, the lowlands; and scattered farmsteads, more useful for the keeping of animals and therefore more prevalent in the uplands.

The rig system of cultivation – narrow strips of land divided annually by lot among the farming community – has come in for much criticism, particularly from the eighteenth-century improvers, who saw it, justifiably, as a barrier to investment, and therefore profit. But when society was primarily organized around the need to sustain the community, it was both sensible and fair as a means of ensuring that everyone shared good and bad land.

From a social point-of-view, medieval people were divided into two fundamental groups: free and unfree. The latter, the serfs, were by no means the poorest in society, but they suffered from the basic economic handicap of not being able to leave their master's estate and the social stigma of passing this unappealing status on to their children. Serfs were property, pure and simple, no matter how well looked after they were, and it shouldn't surprise us to find that many would brave even unfavourable economic conditions to be free.

The vast bulk of the free population encompassed, of course, a range of inequalities. At the very bottom of the heap came landless labourers. At a time of rising population, as was the case in the twelfth and thirteenth centuries, their situation was fairly dire indeed, since manpower was so plentiful and so cheap. However, most of the population did own at least a vegetable patch from which to supply their family's basic needs. Others, well-to-do-farmers, not only cultivated much larger areas of land but hired others to work for them. The downside was the amount of time spent cultivating the estate owner's land, and the plethora of dues and services which he also claimed.

You knew you had arrived in the tiny band of the landed elite when you did not owe labour service to anyone else. Of course, you owed another kind of service, but that carried its own status. However, by the thirteenth century the neat feudal pyramid of service owed ever upwards until it reached the king had caved in somewhat under the weight of overlapping and competing superiorities. Those who could get hold of more land might thereby also acquire a plethora of feudal superiors – those above them in the pyramid. And where did that leave loyalty?

The king had no doubt about the ultimate answer to that question. Feudalism appealed to the leaders of emerging western European kingdoms because it made them the legal focus of both landholding and military service. The long process of forging a nation was undoubtedly helped by this development over the longer term. Certainly, the earls of Scotland, as elsewhere, did not rush to convert their time-honoured, but undocumented, landholding rights into feudal charters. However, the fact that they had done so by 1200 indicates that they did eventually see the benefits for themselves, the most important being protection in law. They also didn't necessarily have much choice.

Having conquered England, the new Norman monarchs there found themselves with an unusual opportunity to rationalize existing systems, as the Domesday Book of the

1180s exemplifies. Many, though not all, of these kings proved committed legislators but above all they liked things neat, tidy and English, in the sense of all-embracing at a national level. In Scotland, national legislation did exist, but kings of Scots knew better than to tamper with all the existing layers of regional law.

However, they did exert stricter control over much of Scotland (excluding the earldoms and other major lordships) through the formal establishment of the sheriffdoms, most of which were in place by the mid-twelfth century. The sheriff was the key royal official at a local level, responsible for bringing in the revenues necessary to maintain the royal household and national government and administering royal justice to the local population. The kind of guys who had once been thanes probably now became sheriffs, though earls could have their own thanes too.

Many of the revolutions associated with Norman influence can be traced to the reign of David I (1124-1153). The youngest son of Malcolm III and his saintly wife Margaret, David had spent his adolescence in England, wher he had considerable lands and where, after 1100, his sister was queen.. As an extensive landowner in Lothian prior to becoming king, this energetic man had already put Norman practices, not to mention Norman friends, in place. Now he could extend this to the kingdom.

But David was no slouch when it came to defending Scottish independence in the face of threats from England and was actually one of the most successful Scottish kings in terms of expanding Scottish territory to the south. Even the setback of the battle of the Standard in 1138, when David first took the field against his former hosts (much to their disgust), failed to dent his enthusiasm for encroaching on the old Northumbrian kingdom. However, that battle, which may have been lost for the Scots by David's decision to allow the wild Galwegian footsoldiers to make the first charge instead of the cavalry, also indicated the limitations of the power of a king of Scots. The general behaviour of the Galwegians, who merely followed their own military traditions, which still included the use of slavery, shocked Norman sensibilities, and not just in the English army. It is no easy task to treat this culture clash even-handedly when most of what we have to deal with is a web of outraged opinion in the one-sided sources.

Coin of David I.

Coin of Henry, earl of Northumberland (1139-1152).

King David succeeded, temporarily at least, in extending Scottish territory down through Cumbria in particular, making Carlisle a Scottish royal base and gaining access to the Cumbrian silver mines which now at last began to produce the first Scottish coins. However, his success was based on temporary English instability caused by the bitter civil war over the succession to King Henry I. Once that had been sorted out, David's own death ensured that the wily Henry II was able to restore the border to its previous position.

The main legacy of David I was perhaps less his secular administrative reforms, though he was certainly active in bringing parts of Lothian and central eastern Scotland in particular up to Norman standards, and more the fact that he actively encouraged the introduction to Scotland of a new dynamic force: the reformed monastic orders. This marked a new phase in the economic, as well as spiritual, development of western Europe.

These new orders, which eventually displaced the Culdees, attracted the attention, and patronage, of the secular elites for a number of reasons, not least the fact that their overt discipline and spiritual rigour promised a much easier passage into heaven for the donor, his family and his ancestors. Such considerations were worth every penny of income from the large gifts of land which men like David lavished on them.

Once they had been given such grants, these monks worked very hard to ensure that few worldly rules and regulations got in the way of ensuring that the land was worked in the most productive way possible. We should not be too cynical about the logic that lay behind the healthy capitalist ideology that seems, to the modern eye, to be lurking behind this monastic activity. The creation of wealth was the most certain road to enabling the monks to put God's purpose for the faithful here on earth into practice. The fact that they, under the direction of the pope in Rome, were the interpreters of that purpose, making the whole process something of a closed shop, did not enter the heads of most of the medieval faithful. We might look back at the thoroughness with which they acted, often forcibly removing current tenants who held particular rights so that the land could be worked by lay brothers solely in the interests of the monastery, with a healthy scepticism. Nevertheless, the example that these monks presented to lay landowners in terms of estate organization and interest in the development of European markets undoubtedly helped to stimulate the Scottish economy.

Sweetheart Abbey.

The ruins of Glenluce Abbey, founded in the twelfth century by the Cistercians.

The main area of economic development in which Scotland came to excel in this period was the wool trade, which fed the much larger and extremely lucrative cloth industry. Before 1300, Scotland could actually claim to be exporting more wool and hides per head of population then England, though this was at the lower quality end of the market. Berwick, Scotland's most important port, was the *entrepôt* for this economic activity, serving the important hinterland of the Border uplands, home to the vast sheep ranches of the great abbeys of the south. The remains of these huge enterprises can still be picked out in the Cheviots.

What is harder to imagine is the hive of industry which these tentative remains represent. As well as just the sheer numbers of sheep (admittedly of a smaller, more hardy breed than the current Dolly lookalikes), the ranches played host to the agents of continental cloth manufacturers who commandeered wool harvests many years in advance. Berwick boasted a number of halls owned and occupied by representatives of the key economic players of western Europe from the Low Countries and the Baltic states.

As with all such economic activity, there were spin-offs for the surrounding area. Roxburgh, one of the most important burghs of the middle ages, owed its prosperity to its role as a gathering point for the wool and as a market for a vast array of fancy goods imported as a result of the healthy state of the area's exports. The middling sort, merchants and wool dealers, grew rich and important within their own communities, beginning to mimic their social superiors in their monastic endowments and the range of quality luxury items which they were able to purchase. It is little wonder that the early thirteenth century in particular was regarded nostalgically by later generations suffering under war and economic setback. This was perhaps not a Golden Age but things were looking rather good for many Scots.

It really did depend on who you were and where you lived. For those living in other parts of the country, immediate concerns were rather different. The cultural independence of the Galwegians has already been mentioned. Elsewhere the desire of the king of Scots to exert his authority over the entire mainland and on towards the western and northern isles put him in direct conflict not only with the independent-minded petty kings of these areas, but with the King of Norway as well.

Norway, as a result of the Viking conquest of much of the north and west right down through the Isle of Man into Ireland, technically owned this vast territory to the west of Alba. A degree of stability was brought to the area in a treaty between King Magnus Barelegs of Norway and King Edgar of Scotland in 1098, which laid down who owned what: Alba/Scotland held the mainland but the western isles remained Norwegian. However, this did not stop later kings of Scots from continuing to push their authority into Norwegian territory.

The leaders of the Norse-Gaelic kingdoms of the west would rather have owed allegiance to no-one but, if they had to choose, generally preferred the king of Norway to the king of Scots, simply because the former was less likely, for geographical reasons, to interfere. The king of (the Isle of) Man was the main powerbroker at the beginning of the new millennium, but dynastic problems of the usual infighting sort gave rise to a split in the Irish Sea world and the ascendancy of a new power, *ri innse gall* – King of the Isles – the most famous of whom was Somerled.

It might be argued that these galley-powered warrior kings were yesterday's men, representatives of an outmoded and violent culture that stood in the way of the inevitable civilizing influence of the Norman-inspired Scottish kings. Such a view is, in itself, extremely old-fashioned. This was, as mentioned before, a clash of cultures, and we should try not to take sides. There is, however, increasing evidence that many west coast nobles cherrypicked aspects of both mainstream Gaelic and mainstream Scottish culture, interacting with the elites of both societies and well beyond.

On the other hand, we must also recognize that the increasing encroachments of Scottish families such as the Stewarts, well known for their active and loyal royal service, was regarded as unwarranted interference by the powerful magnates of the west and north. Indeed, Somerled's final invasion of 1164, which saw the terrible highland galleys enter the Clyde and attack Renfrew, the main seat of the Stewarts, was a direct attempt to try to restrict Scottish influence in the west. Unfortunately, Somerled's death in that engagement is perhaps symbolic of the fact that he was, both literally and metaphorically, fighting a losing battle. Certainly the tendency of these apprehensive west coast magnates to back challengers for the Scottish throne, such as Donald MacWilliam, provided an ideal opportunity for central government, and its historians, to castigate them all as rebels and troublemakers. The story has two sides.

The thirteenth-century kings of Scots wanted their authority in the west to reach its logical conclusion: the complete takeover of the area, either with the acquiescence of the King of Norway or without. Norway's ownership of the western isles had been in danger of becoming merely a technicality until the accession of Haakon IV. This dynamic and successful monarch made strenuous efforts to enforce effective sovereignty over the west

Trinity Temple, North Uist. Tradition has it that the church was founded by the daughter of Somerled, the famous King of the Isles.

highland magnates who were in danger of being absorbed politically by Scotland. Various rebuffed attempts to buy the western isles from Norway in the mid-thirteenth century finally led to a military showdown in 1263.

The battle of Largs of that year was no great Scottish victory, but Haakon's death shortly afterwards paved the way to a sale agreement in 1266. It was now surely only a matter of time until the Gaelic west became fully integrated into the rest of Scotland, as had happened to other 'difficult' areas like Moray and Ross in previous centuries.

Scotland had moved on considerably by 1200 and another major step in identity was being taken around that time, albeit probably only by the literate few. Having already stopped describing his people as the hotchpotch of Gaels, Saxons, Britons, Normans, etc., that they actually were, the king of Scots now began to consider that everyone who owed him allegiance should now view themselves as living in Scotland. Before that time 'Scotland' only referred to the core part of Alba. By the death of Alexander III in 1286, it now included the entire mainland and the western isles as well.

Strong regional identities continued to exist, however, and local power structures exerted more influence over most people's lives than the centre. This strong local focus also found expression in considerable cultural diversity. Some of the earliest Scottish ballads date from these centuries, reflecting a strong interest in folklore and ancient moral and spiritual ideals. They are also firmly rooted in place. The songs and poetry of this period reflect a society which loved to listen to long traumatic tales of love, death, violence and betrayal to while away a cold winter's night. In that respect, little had probably changed for thousands of years, even if the cultural references were constantly updated.

Elite culture was both peculiarly Scottish and part of a wider European scene. The nobility of Scotland was multilingual – speaking in French when mingling at court, but also perfectly able to converse in the native language of the area from which they hailed. Since intermarriage between the Norman newcomers and native aristocrats was the natural next step in the integration process, their offspring were brought up with a mixture of cultural and linguistic influences. They liked to have around them items of the best quality, and, like the rest of the country, to listen to music, songs and poetry that were also a mixture of the peculiarly Scottish and the unashamedly European. They weren't necessarily a terribly literate bunch, but some did enjoy learned society. All in all, one gets a sense of a Scotland that certainly had its problems, but which generally looked forward to the future with confidence.

Which makes it all the more unfortunate that the later thirteenth century proved to be the prelude not to increasingly peaceful and stable conditions (albeit at the expense of self-determination in some parts of the country that resented increased Scottish royal control) but to centuries of bitter war.

SIX

Scotland United?

1286 – 1357

It is almost impossible to imagine Scottish history without the wars of independence; and yet, that is exactly what we must try to do in order to make sense of the period leading up to the outbreak of war in 1296. Despite long-standing claims of English lordship over Scotland, it was unusual in the Europe of the thirteenth century for a nation with an established monarchy and centralized bureaucracy, as opposed to a region or non-centralized kingdom, to be taken over by a neighbouring state.

In addition to thinking the unthinkable, Edward I was also an unusual king of England, in that he combined the sense of God-given superiority which came naturally to his father, Henry III, and his grandfather, John, with obvious administrative *and* military abilities. Nevertheless, conquering Scotland would not have occurred even to the great Longshanks (so called because he was remarkably tall) if circumstances had not brought the northern kingdom to a leaderless situation.

For the fact remains that England and Scotland in the thirteenth century had much in common, while maintaining separate identities. We must try to understand that loyalty in this period was not automatically the prerequisite of the state in which one predominantly lived. It belonged most properly to the individual (in fact, more often the individuals) to whom one had sworn homage and fealty, the traditional oaths of allegiance to a superior

91

lord. The issue becomes even more complicated when one remembers that kings themselves swore homage and fealty to others. It was a by-product of the increasing emphasis on ideals of kingship and definitions of the state that these potentially contradictory loyalties would come to be tested more and more frequently.

The issue of overlordship – the assertion that the English crown held superior rights over the Scottish crown, and therefore over Scotland itself – was, of course, a key element in the lead-up to war and the theoretical justification for it. However, before we go any further, it is important to make clear firstly that both sides believed equally strongly that their position was both rightful and justifiable and secondly that to worry unduly about the legal ins and outs of it would tend to miss the point.

It must surely be doubted whether the Scots, even if their recent kings had sworn homage and fealty to the English king for Scotland, would have chosen not to go to war in defence of the actual independence of the kingdom. Edward I's demands, while legally justifiable in strictly feudal terms, were so blatantly above and beyond anything that had previously been demanded of a king on behalf of his kingdom that a violent reaction was only to be expected. It is also possible, but far more speculative, that Edward I would have found some other excuse – perhaps the threat to the stability of his northern border – to invade once the full extent of the dynastic crisis after the death of Alexander III became obvious. So far as the English were concerned, the major problem with Scotland was the fact that it was a potential ally of their most deadly enemy, France.

All the same, let's take a look at the issue of overlordship as it had come to be understood in the later thirteenth century. Back in the mists of time – or at least before the Norman conquest of England in 1066 – we can point to a number of occasions when kings of the embryonic Scotland had admitted that they ranked lower down the scale of kingship than Saxon kings of what was rapidly becoming England. This was, of course, forced out of them as a result of temporary military defeat, most famously at the battle of Brunanburh near the Humber in 937. Gradations of kingship were commonplace at that time and didn't necessarily make any difference to actual authority.

As noted in Chapter Five, the essential problem lay in the fact that the boundaries between the two kingdoms were still in the process of being fixed. By the eleventh century, the Scottish kings were very keen to move the border further south to take in more of the old Saxon kingdom of Northumbria. With the Norman conquest, the situation became more legalistic, but was still based on whether or not the Scottish kings could be forced into an acknowledgement of their inferiority after a military defeat. Unfortunately, in all cases, they managed to get themselves into that situation by invading England in the first place. The first instance took place in 1072 when King William 'the Conqueror' of England finally took revenge on Malcolm III of Scotland for both provocatively marrying a princess of the exiled Saxon royal family and invading the north of England two years previously. Malcolm dutifully went through the formal ceremony of performing homage and fealty to William, though this did not stop him from invading England on two further occasions.

There was one other important factor in the overlordship debate and that was the role of the English church, which, at least as much as the monarchy, was responsible for developing and maintaining the idea of a Scotland ultimately subject to English authority. The reason behind this deeply ingrained belief was again historical, originating in the struggle by the archbishops of York to maintain their authority against their rivals in Canterbury, using Scottish bishops to help them. In 1192, the Scottish church, losing patience, sought papal help, resulting in official daughter status, 'no-one in between', being formally established between Scotland (excluding Galloway, which still formall acknowledged the authority of York) and Rome.

However, the English church had not lost the battle completely, succeeding most notably in preventing the Scottish king in the thirteenth century from acquiring the precious right to crowning and anointing (the ultimate symbol of kingship) by reminding the pope that the English kings claimed overlordship over Scotland. There was still everything to play for, for both sides.

On 19 March 1286, Alexander III of Scotland died at the age of forty-six, a respectable enough age for a medieval monarch even if his departure was unexpected, to say the least. (Falling off his horse during a passionate dash to see his new young queen was perhaps not the most dignified of ends for the last of the MacMalcolm kings.) Unfortunately, and despite an attempt to deal with the succession question after the death of his only surviving son in 1284, Alexander's only potential direct heir, his three-year old granddaughter Margaret, the Maid of Norway, faced a disturbed path to the empty throne. The Maid's great-uncle, Edward I, was called upon by Scotland's senior statesmen to help the country in its hour of need, especially in view of the threat of civil war presented by Robert Bruce, lord of Annandale, known as the Competitor because of his tirelessly proactive campaign to gain the throne.

Nevertheless, the Scottish nobility, despite exhibiting the deeply factionalist tendencies natural to most political animals, managed to promote a degree of stability in much, if not all, parts of the country. They chose from among them (a considerable feat in itself) six

Coin of Alexander III, whose death in 1286 left a power vacuum in Scotland.

Edward I of England as represented on his royal seal.

guardians, representatives of the main social, geographical and political groupings, to assume control of government and maintain links with the outside world.

The Scottish leaders continued to act, on balance, with as much farsightedness and common sense as the limited available options made possible, agreeing to a marriage between the Maid and Edward's son and heir, but with firm guarantees of Scotland's continuing independence. The death of the little princess, *en route* to Scotland, in 1290 unravelled several years of hard work on all sides and made the horrifying prospect of all-out civil war even more likely.

The contest for the throne – which revolved round two candidates, the bellicose octogenarian Robert Bruce and John Balliol, lord of Galloway and Barnard Castle – could have been settled either in the law courts or on the battlefield. Fortunately for Scotland, the former was a viable option. Unfortunately, Edward I was in pole position to act as judge, with a new and important caveat: he must be acknowledged as overlord of Scotland. The Scottish leaders reacted with shock and consternation and did not, *en masse*, give Edward what he wanted. Unfortunately, the candidates – there were now twelve – were individually prepared to swear homage and fealty, effectively deciding the issue. John Balliol, who had the support of the most important political family in Scotland, the Comyns, tried hard to avoid this, believing, quite rightly, that he would be chosen as king. Eventually, however, even he bowed to the inevitable.

The seventeen-month Great Cause, as this long drawn-out legal contest was known, gave Edward I ample opportunity to act effectively as the ruler of Scotland and to gather evidence in support of his right to do so. There was little the Scots could do to retaliate: they protested when they could, but, without a king, more dramatic concerted action was unthinkable. Finally, on 17 November 1292, John Balliol was adjudged the rightful king of Scots, but then was forced to swear homage and fealty to Edward not just once but twice.

During John's troubled three-year reign, his attempts to wriggle free of the legal knot that Edward was drawing tight proved futile. Appeals from the Scottish king's court to Westminster and the threat of Scottish military service *en masse* in an English army against France made it clear that overlordship was no longer an annoying but merely technical sign of weakness. According to the medieval Scottish chroniclers, John himself finally lost patience and summoned his own parliament, which agreed that homage and fealty should be withdrawn.

The Scots knew better than to appeal to Edward's better nature and chose the one course of action that would both widen the chances of a successful breakaway bid and absolutely guarantee war: they concluded a treaty with France in the winter of 1295-6. Edward also didn't wait any longer, sending out orders to muster an English army for March 1296 by the end of 1295. War, finally, was the only option.

To begin with, the Scots displayed a near-suicidal optimism, invading England and even daring to engage an English army. Edward himself began by slaughtering most of the citizens of Berwick for their audacious resistance. The Scottish balloon was then completely burst at Dunbar on 27 April, when the earl of Surrey's army performed a deft 'make-it-look-like-we're-retreating' manoeuvre, leading to the rout of the Scottish army. A relentless tide of capitulation swiftly followed, right up to the ritual humiliation of King John in July. Scotland was finally under direct English control, surely the last move in a long and tortuous chess game begun (even if the Scots hadn't known it) at least as far back as 1291.

Scotland's misery in 1296 was symbolized by the empty space under the coronation chair – Edward I had seized the revered Stone of Scone and removed it to Westminster, where it remainedunder this throne for 700 years.

With its king and noble leaders in prison in England, its castles garrisoned with English troops and an English government installed in Berwick, the autumn and winter of 1296-7 was surely one of the bleakest in Scotland's history. But Edward had overdone it and he was a fool to think that his six-month tour of Scotland meant the end of resistance. After an initial shock-induced acquiescence in taxation for the English king's next venture against France, tax-resistance and general recalcitrance against the alien government took hold in almost every part of Scotland. By spring 1297, Scotland was no longer paying the wages of its English administrators and England embarked on the long and painful experience of paying for its intrusion into Scotland.

Resistance was spontaneous and uncoordinated. All over Scotland the middle layer of society proved willing and able to organize action against the outrageous financial demands newly falling on them particularly. William Wallace seems to have come from exactly this kind of background: unrecorded in terms of medieval national government (and, hence, history) but important within local power structures. These men were not afraid to speak their minds and act in defence of their families and communities.

Having hit the headlines in south-west Scotland, followed by a lightning but targeted attack on the English justiciar (a senior legal officer) at Scone – a direct hit at English government – Wallace moved into the safety of Selkirk forest in the south-east to plan and train his men. By now, Wallace was no longer working on his own; the Scottish nobility, some now released from prison, could see how the war should be fought. Wallace was soon put in touch with arguably the most successful rebellion of this period, certainly in terms of getting rid of English garrisons – the northern revolt under Andrew Murray and the burgesses of Inverness.

King Edward had other things on his mind, such as his imminent war against France, and made it clear to his officials that these little local difficulties should be dealt with once and for all. The news that Murray and Wallace had joined forces persuaded the Berwick government that they must act quickly against these nobodies to restore their authority.

Murray and Wallace's army was moving south from Dundee, so the English came north to meet them at the inevitable crossing of the Forth at Stirling. The defeat inflicted on Surrey's army on 11 September 1297 by this rag, tag and bobtail force sent shock waves throughout England, though it cost the Scots the life of Andrew Murray.

But Stirling Bridge was no more likely to have ended the war than Edward's own victory campaign of 1296. Ironically, the Scots' very success in defeating Surrey ensured that they would endure the indefinite attentions of a united England. The year 1297 had seen Edward perilously close to pushing his own barons to civil war with his endless demands to fund his military activities. The severe battering done to English national pride at Stirling was perhaps the only thing guaranteed to bring Edward's political community to heel behind their king.

That Wallace was defeated the following year at Falkirk by the Plantagenet himself is perhaps no surprise. The Scottish guardian had prepared well, but neither the Scottish spearmen nor the pathetic numbers of Scottish cavalry were any match for the relentless barrage of arrows despatched by the English archers.

A patriotic (if not necessarily true to life) later representation of William Wallace.

With Wallace discredited, Scottish government, which this time did not collapse with military defeat, rested in the hands of the representatives of competing political factions: John Comyn of Badenoch and Robert Bruce, earl of Carrick. The war now settled down into a rather miserable cycle of English campaigns squeezing more territory from the Scots and Scottish counter-attacks pressing English resources ever more fiercely. Although the balance of resources undoubtedly still lay with England, Scotland also achieved considerable success in the war of words engaged throughout the courts of Europe, and most particularly in Rome. In 1299 King John was released from English prison into papal custody and in 1301 he was effectively permitted to seek the opportunity to return to Scotland, preferably with a French army. The Scots had everything to hope for.

However, it soon became clear that King John would not be coming home. The political situation in Europe had changed and, almost overnight, the Scots found themselves, for reasons which had nothing to do with their own cause, ditched by both the pope and the French king by the end of 1301. This helped to stimulate the increasing acceptance by 'the middling sort' in English-occupied southern Scotland of the necessary evil of Edwardian government in the absence of an alternative. These same people who had objected so strongly to the English presence in 1297 now felt that the interests of their families and communities would no longer be served by indefinite warfare.

Resistance did not collapse immediately. But as Edward conducted yet another large-scale campaign in 1303, crossing the Forth for the first time since 1296, theScots were running out of room for manoeuvre. The guardian, Sir John Comyn, sued for peace on behalf of the people of Scotland. They had done their best and Edward acknowledged as much with reasonably lenient peace terms, guaranteeing not only basic property rights but also a place in government, however limited, for the Scottish nobility. With no king and no diplomatic support, it was time for the Scots to start planning for the future.

For those who argued against this pragmatic line, the most obvious of whom was Sir William Wallace, Edward had no mercy. The execution of Wallace in August 1305 was meant to draw a line under proceedings and in the short term, as Scotland struggled to recover, it probably did. But time was on Scotland's, not Edward's side. It was also an ally of Robert Bruce, earl of Carrick.

We should be careful, when dealing with the future king, not to employ hindsight. From 1300 onwards the Bruce star had been well and truly eclipsed within Scottish politics and, with the arrival of the Comyns back in the English fold, Edward was happy to use that family's political influence to settle Scotland rather than encourage any regal ambitions in Carrick. Everyone, English and Scots, could look forward to a bit of peace and Edward, at sixty-five, might also have welcomed life at a more sedate pace.

But these plans were brought to nought through the overwhelming, driving ambition of Carrick himself (surely inherited undiluted from his grandfather). Goodness knows

Caerlaverock Castle was held by the Maxwell family but was taken by Edward I in his Galloway campaign of 1300. It is a sign of his accommodating peace terms (or his weakness) that Sir Eustace Maxwell was still allowed to keep his castle.

A reconstructed trebuchet at Caerlaverock Castle. The castle was besieged twice by Edward I – in 1300 and again in 1312, when Maxwell declared for Robert Bruce.

what the meeting in the Greyfriar's church at Dumfries in February 1306 betweenCarrick and his bitter rival, John Comyn, was designed to achieve but the end result – the murder of Comyn – precipitated a course of action through which Bruce, and Scotland, had everything to gain. And everything to lose.

Many Scots would surely have contemplated accepting Bruce as king eventually, once the country had had time to recover and the new, voluntary oaths of loyalty to Edward I had been rendered null and void by the latter's surely not-too-distant demise. But the brutal and sacrilegious murder of Comyn forced Bruce to seize the throne immediately, as the only option available to save even his life from the wrath of the dead man's family. It also made supporting him quite impossible for most decent Scots.

So only the most committed of Bruce supporters, like the earl of Atholl and the bishop of Glasgow, headed inevitably to Scone, the ancient inauguration site, for a hurried ceremony on 25 March 1306. Within months even this must have seemed comparatively glorious as the new king was hounded west out of his kingdom. It required a remarkable spirit indeed to survive the deprivations of this exile, along with the terrible news of the execution or imprisonment of so many of his family and supporters.

This time King Edward gave full vent to the terrible Plantagenet rage which had already earned criticism for the treatment of Berwick in 1296. Edward's almost pathological attitude towards continued Scottish resistance undoubtedly helped to engender some sympathy towards King Hobbe, as the English so dismissively described the new king of Scots.

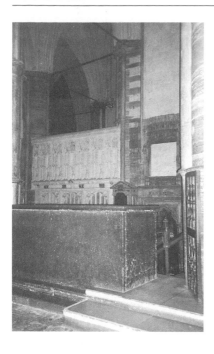

Left: The tomb of Edward I Plantagenet, king of England.

Right: The effigy in Gloucester Cathedral of Edward II, who inherited the English crown in 1307.

Most importantly of all, Bruce benefited enormously from the implications of the death of the great warrior, Edward I, in July 1307. The new English king, the touchy but politically inept Edward II, was both unwilling and unable – thanks not least to the debts he inherited from his father – to provide effective leadership for the war in Scotland, however happy he was to see it continue. The underfunded English presence in Scotland grew more and more unpopular with even their pro-Comyn allies and was rarely able to take the initiative against Bruce.

King Robert I, on the other hand, used the momentum of his early hit-and-run successes against his enemies, increasingly presenting himself as the champion not only of an independent Scotland but of individual interest groups – 'middling folk', churchmen, nobles who had lost out in the settlement of 1304-5, highland magnates – which otherwise had little in common.

But that should not obscure the fact that Bruce faced a far greater problem than the English in the first few tentative years of his reign. The eventuality that the Scottish political community had tried so hard to avoid in the 1280s and '90s had finally, and perhaps predictably, come to a head in a bitter civil war. The long-standing role of the Comyn family at the heart of Scottish government, combined with their close bond with their relation, the ousted King John, and the desire for revenge, made this fight both personal and profoundly political at the same time. The death or exile of the key players on either side alone could resolve it.

Fortunately for Bruce, the Comyns had never displayed any outstanding talent in military matters. Bruce himself, after a rather dodgy start at the battle of Methven, had quickly matured into a cunning and effective guerrilla leader, qualities that mattered far more to Scotland's interests than playing by the established rules. The new king was also blessed with an ability to attract and sustain a close-knit team of military commanders who, happily, were as effective in military terms as their leader. As a result, Bruce could maintain a war on more than one front, sending his only surviving brother, Edward, and the enthusiastic James Douglas down into Galloway to deal with Balliol supporters there, while he himself tackled the Comyn heartland in Lochaber, Badenoch and Buchan.

By 1309 the Comyns were in exile in England and Bruce felt it was now worthwhile calling his first parliament. This important occasion also marked the first concerted effort on the part of the royal propaganda machinery to swing into action to justify the activities of King Robert. The so-called Declaration of the Clergy was sent to the pope by a number of Scottish churchmen to make sense of the apparent about-turn by the Scottish independence movement which had hitherto worked for the reinstatement of King John. This is the only document produced during the entire reign of King Robert which actually refers to his predecessor, kick-starting the myth that John was an English puppet. The reason for John's subsequent expurgation from Scottish history as written by Bruce is entirely understandable. Bruce credentials to be king had not triumphed in court over Balliol's in 1291; it was therefore far easier for King Robert to deal with that unfortunate genealogical fact by

Brass of Robert Bruce, Dunfermline Abbey. Above his shoulders are, on the left, the lion rampant of Scotland and, on the right, the saltire of the Bruce family (also shown right).

*Robert Bruce, in a
seventeenth-century
engraving.*

*Bruce's allies – the arms of (left to right) his brother Edward, Sir James Douglas and Walter Fitzalan, the Steward
(Stewart), whose descendants were to play such a great part in Scottish history.*

portraying himself explicitly as the successor to King Alexander and encouraging everyone to forget about John altogether.

Scotland was not yet entirely King Robert's, despite a series of devastatingly successful attacks on various Scottish castles still in English/Comyn hands. By 1313, though, Bruce felt confident enough to deliver an ultimatum to those members of the Scottish elites who still sat on the fence: swear allegiance to me within a year or lose your lands in Scotland. This certainly upped the ante in a war where this kind of dogmatic attitude towards loyalty had not been seen since Edward I. In reality, Bruce continued to maintain a generally pragmatic attitude towards the confused rump of the Scottish nobility who remained unsure as to how to act towards a murdering usurper who nonetheless had managed to re-establish Scotland as a viable independent entity.

Unfortunately, this ultimatum coincided with an unusual period of English domestic calm and Edward II resolved to re-establish his own political stock within England and give Bruce a run for his money by means of a concerted Scottish campaign. The agreement made between the garrison commander at Stirling and Edward Bruce – that the castle would be handed over to the Scots unless relieved by the English – became the specific issue over which the two armies might potentially fight. It was not, contrary to popular belief, the cause of King Edward's new-found zeal for Scotland.

The battle of Bannockburn, like that of Stirling Bridge (and for the same reason), holds a hugely important place in the collective memory of Scotland: for the second time in a generation the underdogs triumphed against the might of an imperialist military machine.

Right: The handle of the Hawthornden sword, which, like most of the medieval swords of Scotland, is reputed to have been wielded by Robert Bruce. The handle is made from a narwhal tusk and the guards are bent towards the blade to prevent the antagonist's sword from glancing off towards the bearer.

Below: An iron battle-axe head discovered on the battlefield of Bannockburn. It was with an axe such as this that Bruce killed Henry de Bohun, nephew of the earl of Hereford.

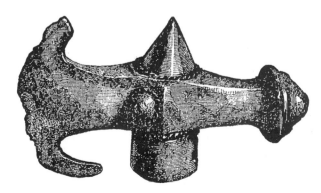

The Scottish king, quite rightly, seems to have thought long and hard about actually committing to battle – perhaps he had a personal memory of Wallace making a similar decision to fight at Falkirk. It was only Scottish successes in a series of skirmishes on the first day (21 June 1314), combined with news of the profound problems of leadership and low morale in the English army that finally persuaded him. The resulting victory, caused partly by the deliberate fencing in of the deadly English archers, sealed King Robert's fame in military matters for all time and also gave him a far securer mandate to rule within Scotland. The 1313 ultimatum could be put into immediate effect and many waverers finally accepted the reality of a Bruce kingship.

What Bannockburn did not do, however, was win the war. The failure to capture Edward himself rendered the victory only partial in strictly military terms: the younger English king needed only to sit tight and refuse to acknowledge Scottish independence to ensure that the Scottish king spent the rest of his life in insecurity and military activity.

And indeed Bruce's great victory prompted, if anything, an even greater obsession with England. The practice of invading over the border and extorting blackmail from the local inhabitants for the privilege of not being burnt out had begun even before Bannockburn, but it was developed into a fine art in succeeding years. The corresponding loss of revenue to the English treasury must have annoyed Edward but the suffering of the area made little impact on the southern-based English government.

Bruce's need to extract an admission by England of Scotland's sovereign status was a product both of an awareness of his own mortality – the deprivations of his early years seem to have had a profound effect on his health – and the lack of a direct Bruce heir. Thanks to Bannockburn, his wife, Queen Elizabeth, was released from English captivity. But there can be little doubt that the succession issue – the very one that had precipitated the war in the first place – not only left King Robert with an insecurity complex but also prompted an interest in a man who was both adult and the son of a Scottish king: Edward Balliol.

Believe it or not, the king's own political stock within Scotland took a significant dive only a few years after Bannockburn, partly as a result of the continuing failure to bring an end to the war. In 1315, typical Bruce lateral thinking prompted an ambitious scheme designed to force King Edward to accept him as king of an independent Scotland, given the ultimate failure of the raids into England on that score. Unfortunately the invasion of Ireland (owned by England by this time) and the setting-up of Edward Bruce as High King in the Emerald Isle coincided with a series of Europe-wide bad harvests and an outbreak of cattle disease. The native Irish, suspicious of the imposition of a central authority at the best of times, came to hate the Scots as much as the English as the invading army used up increasingly scarce foodstuffs.

The raids in England had at least provided the Scottish war chest with an unprecedented and reasonably regular income. Ireland proved that the Bruces were not invincible. The campaigns, some of which were led directly by King Robert, were both inglorious and miserable. The fact that the Scottish king was prepared to risk both his own life and that of his designated heir, his brother Edward, on this venture must also have forced the Scottish political community to realize that Scotland's best interests might still

The old road to England, highway for Scottish raiders in the years after Bannockburn.

come second to those of the Bruce dynasty. The death of Edward Bruce in October 1318 finally put an end to this military fiasco but it was surely no coincidence that a parliament later in the year had to passed measure to curb those who muttered openly against the government.

It was not all doom and gloom, however. In 1318 the Scots finally managed to reclaim Berwick, the last outpost of English-held Scotland. Unfortunately, this was done at the cost of ignoring papal efforts to stop the fighting between Scotland and England so that a Crusade could be organized. The price was excommunication of the whole country. This was the context in which the Declaration of Arbroath, that most resounding of assertions of independence to be found anywhere, was sent to Rome in 1320, ostensibly by the Scottish nobility but most certainly at the instigation of the king. In the longer-term, the papacy did come to accept both Bruce as king and Scotland's independence, *de facto* (in reality) and *de jure* (by right). But the most immediate result of this remarkable piece of propaganda was to spark off a plot against King Robert.

The Soules conspiracy, so-called because its leader was the hereditary butler, Sir William Soules, was most certainly not about placing William on the throne, as most versions would have it – why then would Soules have been spared execution? The key to the conspiracy actually lay outside Scotland with the arrival at the English court of Edward Balliol, another ace now held by Edward II. This prompted a number of pro-Balliol/Comyn supporters who had reluctantly accepted Bruce as king out of political necessity after Bannockburn to seek to revive the infinitely more legitimate Balliol kingship. And presumably the general climate of dissatisfaction with the Bruce government in the aftermath of the Ireland fiasco and in the light of the imminent papal interdict convinced the conspirators that there would be a widespread desire for a change of regime.

The fact that they were wrong (or perhaps that Bruce was fortunate enough to hear of their activities in time) should not blind us to the fact that this whole episode provides unequivocal evidence that the king's position, fourteen years into his reign, was far from assured. On the other hand, this very insecurity should perhaps make us realize just how impressive Bruce's achievements actually were, in the face of continuing and genuine opposition. The aging king (he was nearly fifty) was also now prepared to accept that his policies had failed to move him any closer to a permanent settlement with England. In 1323 he agreed a thirteen-year truce with Edward, which, crucially, would remain in force with the death of either monarch. This was the best that Bruce, who surely expected to die first, could hope for.

But he was clearly born beneath a lucky star as circumstances beyond Scotland once more conspired to bring success within King Robert's grasp. The deposition and murder of Edward II in 1327 was too good an opportunity for Bruce to miss, despite the 1323 treaty stipulating that peace should continue into the next reign: the Scots streamed over the border yet again, this time threatening to annex parts of the north of England. The regency government in England took the short-term option and sought peace with King Robert.

The treaty of Northampton-Edinburgh, concluded in 1328, provided a categorical acceptance of both Bruce's kingship and Scotland's sovereign status, as well as heralding a marriage between Bruce's four-year old son, David, and the new English king's sister, Joan, and the payment of £20,000 by the Scots. Perhaps the treaty can be criticized for failing to accommodate the long-standing grievances of those, both Scots and English, who had lost lands as a result of Bruce's seizure of the throne in 1306. However, we must surely acknowledge that getting the treaty at all was a dream come true for both Bruce and Scotland. Besides, it is hard to see how these grievances could have been dealt with considering that these lands were now occupied by Bruce supporters who surely would have been at least as bitter about being turfed out at this stage.

Perhaps of more significance was the fact that the young King Edward III, together with the overwhelming body of English opinion, remained publicly disgusted with the whole agreement. But Edward was not yet in power and even his non-attendance at his sister's wedding presumably failed to blight the last year of Bruce's reign. King Robert, whose determination alone had seen him through the campaigns of 1327 in the face of deteriorating health, effectively retired from public life to his new manor at Cardross on Lochlomondside. He died, having secured his throne, his kingdom and his dynasty, in June 1329. The question of how long it would last would have to be answered by others.

King Robert had planned the future beyond his death with his customary long-term strategic planning. The guardian for the young King David was Thomas Randolph, earl of Moray, Bruce's nephew and most trusted commander, a man of sense and authority. Unfortunately for Scotland he too was dead by 1332. Equally unfortunate was the fact that

The Bruce immortalized: King Robert's memorial statue at Stirling, perennial battleground throughout Scottish history.

Scottish knights are interspersed with the evangelists on the fifteenth-century Bruce cenotaph.

Edward III had now assumed full power and was determined not only to avenge the insult on his kingship which the 1328 treaty represented but, like his grandfather, to break the Franco-Scottish alliance, which Bruce had renewed in 1326, through outright conquest of the northern kingdom. Like Edward I, the young English king's main focus of attention was France rather than Scotland, not least because he had a claim to the disputed French throne through his mother.

Initially King Edward sought to maintain the letter of the law in relation to the Anglo-Scottish treaty by encouraging the disinherited, the most important of whom was still Edward Balliol, to take the initiative against Scotland. Not that they needed much encouragement, particularly the claimant to the defunct Comyn earldom of Buchan, Sir Henry Beaumont.

Balliol and his motley crew of Anglo-Scots landed in Fife in August 1332. The Bruce forces, lacking effective leadership at this crucial moment, were routed at Dupplin, south-west of Perth and just over a month later Scone witnessed its second coronation within a year as King Edward Balliol ascended his father's throne. Unfortunately, unlike King John, this Balliol embraced subordinate kingship, swearing homage and fealty to Edward III at Roxburgh a few months later. To add injury to insult, he granted the English king the whole of southern Scotland at the same time.

Edward III could pretend no longer and made his war with Scotland official. By May 1334 King David and Queen Joan were in France for their own safety. The Bruce cause was looking increasingly desperate and Scotland itself suffered dreadfully under a war of deliberate destruction. But once again this policy of repression backfired against the English king. Succeeding a series of inept guardians, the son of Wallace's comrade-in-arms at Stirling Bridge, another and equally effective Andrew Murray, was able to begin to turn the tables. Edward Balliol doubtless tried hard to become an effective ruler but was fundamentally hoisted by the petard of his relationship with Edward III. Scotland had come too far down the road of anti-English feeling to back a king who had no loyalty to his kingdom, however legitimate his claim.

Scotland's relationship with France also helped in the struggle for survival, although this was certainly not a question of direct French aid. The outbreak of what became known as the Hundred Years War between England and France in 1337, combined with increasing Scottish success in turning hostilities yet again into a costly war of attrition, forced Edward III to choose which war he wished to actively pursue. In 1341 David Bruce was able to return to his kingdom where he soon showed himself keen to lead from the front. Even his capture at Neville's Cross in 1346 failed to push English policy beyond the maintenance of the border against Scottish attack. Scottish government rested in the hands of David's nephew and heir, Robert Stewart, who, together with his ally William Lord Douglas, began to build up an alternative power bloc to the absent Bruce king.

However, the difficult relationship between King David, who returned to Scotland with a huge ransom to pay in 1357, and the Steward was a reflection of a changing Scottish political climate. The extended royal family could only get away with such infighting because the war with England was no longer the overriding political issue.

Edward III and his family, from frescoes in St Stephen's Chapel, Westminster (now destroyed). Left to right: Thomas of Woodstock, duke of Gloucester; Edward III; Philippa of Hainault; Edward the Black Prince.

Bothwell Castle was taken by Edward III in 1336 and became the English headquarters in Scotland.

From now on England made little more than occasional half-hearted gestures towards acting on their continuing claims of overlordship. On the other hand, Edward Balliol's foolish gift of southern Scotland to Edward III ensured that the kings of Scots spent the next century trying to recover large swathes of the country and one king, James II, inadvertently lost his life in the attempt. The eventual union of the Crowns of Scotland and England can perhaps be seen as a by-product of the war. The marriage between James IV of Scotland and Margaret Tudor in 1503 (which brought James VI of Scotland to the throne of England 100 years later) was certainly an attempt to build the kind of bridges that would not have been necessary without the bitter legacy of the previous 200 years of Anglo-Scottish history.

By that time, Scottish identity had long been defined predominantly in terms of not being English, as it so often is today. The wars had forced one particular answer to issues of loyalty and identity, while also continuing to ask serious questions of those in parts of Scotland, like the west highlands, who did not see supporting the Scottish crown as necessarily their duty. Ultimately the wars between Scotland and England had repercussions for many aspects of Scotland's domestic and foreign policy: it took over two hundred years before a closer relationship between the two countries could even be contemplated. There was no turning the clock back: this was a new Scotland, harder and meaner, perhaps, but also confident and outward-looking – so long as it wasn't to England.

SEVEN

Scotland Revealed

1357 – 1542

The wars with England were clearly a vitally important milestone in Scottish history, but there is a danger of overemphasizing their significance over the longer term. At first glance, it does seem logical to conclude that the seemingly constant stravaiging of soldiers from both sides over a land now geared primarily for war and not economic development was surely bad news for Scotland. In the short term, in some parts of the country, particularly the war zone of the south, life was undoubtedly hard, with some estates showing returns of only a fifth of their pre-war totals (though this is based on extremely limited evidence). So, many Scots experienced great hardship, helping to foster a profound bitterness against England that coloured politics for many centuries to come. Mind you, the north of England reciprocated the feeling after their experiences of intensive Scottish raiding over the border.

However, for much of the half century after 1296, most of Scotland was not directly involved in warfare, and life under a Scottish administration of some kind was perfectly possible, to a greater or lesser extent. To be blunt, wider economic changes affecting Europe as a whole had a far greater impact on Scotland's prosperity over the medium- to long-term. After 1300, the climate began to deteriorate, becoming colder and wetter. The population, which had increased dramatically before that date, forcing families onto more and more undesirable land, had started to contract long before the plague outbreaks of the later fourteenth century began their prolific dance of death. Nevertheless, Scotland probably did not suffer the extremes of growth and contraction associated with this period in the same way as more densely-populated parts of Europe (though again the evidence is very patchy).

So, it would be wrong to presume that the effects of war, even including the loss of that great trading centre, Berwick, until the mid-fifteenth century, were catastrophic. The ramifications of this terrible conflict lay far more in the political sphere than the economic one. It is tempting to see one of the main lessons of the wars of independence for king and political community as being the fundamental need to keep the royal dynasty safe and sound – for the obvious reason that that's how the whole stramash had come about in the first place. However, as we shall see, this is not the same as saying that the political community would permit the king to do exactly as he pleased.

Another important aspect of the wars was actually more of a side-effect, but a significant one nevertheless. As we saw in Chapter Five, Scotland formally acquired the western highlands and islands in 1266, only thirty years before Edward I invaded. If a strong Scottish kingship supported by ambitious Scottish noble families had continued after the death of Alexander III, there can be little doubt that the region, like so many before, would eventually have become fully integrated into Scottish political life, however reluctantly. Ironically, the wars, so important to Scottish identity and unity in other ways, inadvertently helped to create a major political divide north and south of the highland line.

In part this was because west highland magnates were able to exploit the fact that the Scottish crown had more important things on its mind, like its very survival after 1296, and so could play their own regional politics largely unhindered. This revolved mainly around a struggle for dominance of the area between the MacDougall and MacDonald families: if one supported the Scottish crown, the other tended to do the opposite.

The hiatus in strong central authority in Scotland also left them free to absorb the changes taking place in Gaeldom across the Irish Sea, transforming west highland society into a far more overtly militarized culture where the warrior became the main social and economic unit. If they had just stuck to their own part of the world, perhaps this wouldn't have mattered too much (for the moment!). However, the interests of the MacDonalds, who had won the internal leadership struggle by the later fourteenth century, took them east, up the Great Glen towards Moray and the plains of Aberdeen. There they inevitably came into close contact with lowlanders, who took grave exception to the protection rackets basically being run by the highlanders. And so, for the first time, we hear the indignant voice of outraged lowland Scottish opinion, through the chronicler John of Fordun, castigating the western ruffians for violent, unruly and savage behaviour, though apparently they were really rather handsome!

The later fourteenth century has, until recently, remained something of a no-go area, filled with nondescript kings and precious little excitement until the arrival on the scene of the unpleasant but powerful King James I in 1424. Much of the blame for this apparent tediousness used to be placed firmly on the shoulders of King Robert Bruce's successors, his son, David II, his nephew, the first Stewart king, Robert II, followed by Robert III. But we're not nearly so harsh on them these days.

David II faced two related problems. The first was his enforced stay in England between 1346 and 1357 after his capture at the battle of Neville's Cross; the second was the emergence of his nephew and heir, Robert Stewart, together with the latter's ally, the increasingly powerful earl of Douglas, as key political figures in Scotland.

In some ways, it was the establishment of the Douglases that proved most indicative of longer-term trends. The family had risen to prominence through the relationship between the Good Sir James and Robert Bruce, and royal service continued to be their watchword. However, that service was now fundamentally associated with protecting the border, either in peace, or, more usually, in war. Scotland's domestic and foreign policy now revolved round the existence of a cold war with England and that profoundly altered the political balance within the northern kingdom. The old Alba, with its heartland north of the Forth even in the thirteenth century, was no longer the dominant part. Now Scotland south of the Forth-Clyde line, looking hawkishly south, began to take the lead, with the earl of Douglas out in front.

When David returned in 1357, there was no real royal party left in Scotland, and this was something he sought to remedy as quickly as possible. He didn't always make friends on the way to re-establishing his authority, and the nobility often grumbled at his unwarranted interference, for which we should perhaps read the king doing anything at all. David was interested in firm government, regularizing and tightening up procedures, but he generally seems to have known when he was in danger of offending too many vested interests. This was to remain a key theme in crown-magnate relations for the next centuries and some kings got it badly wrong.

David was also fortunate, given that he had an annual ransom of 10,000 merks (about £6,700) to pay over ten years for his freedom, that his reign saw trade pick up throughout

Coin of David II.

Europe, meaning that he received more from the customs. He also managed to demand increasing amounts. The burghs, which paid these taxes, naturally wanted extra bargaining power in return and became an official component in royal government when David finally asked them to attend parliament regularly as the third estate.

David died childless in 1371 and, much to his surprise, Robert Stewart found himself with a crown. Like his uncle, the new king realized the importance of establishing a firm political base from which an erstwhile noble family could wield the power of a monarch. Fortunately for him, but unfortunately for the dynasty in the long run, Robert, unlike David, had no trouble at all in producing children and thus the Stewarts acquired a plethora of earldoms and links to the major Scottish noble families through their marriages.

Robert II, though in his fifties when he became king, was not yet ready to retire. From his point of view, his marriage policy worked – even the MacDonald lord of the Isles became a son-in-law and proved more cooperative than in subsequent reigns. When real trouble appeared, it came from within the dynasty itself but it seems unfair to place too much blame on the first Stewart king for seeking to establish himself by creating a royal family firm.

It was also not Robert II's fault that his own son and heir, the future Robert III, was incapacitated by a kick from a horse and that his second son, another Robert, earl of Fife and later Duke of Albany, would eventually challenge the eldest branch of the family for power. But the key question is not who did what to whom, and what this says about royal power in medieval Scotland, but whether all this royal infighting really made much difference to the lives of most Scots.

We have already mentioned that power in Scotland was heavily uncentralized. It therefore follows that, so long as the basic power structures beyond the centre continued to operate successfully, royal squabbling would prove make or break, in terms of power and fortune, for only a very few within the close royal circle. This does not mean that the king himself was an irrelevant figurehead: he remained the lynchpin of the nation, its identity and good governance. A classic example of what happened when there was an imbalance in these concentric power structures revolved round the activities of Alexander, the 'Wolf' of Badenoch, Robert II's third son.

In the last years of his father's reign, Alexander joined his brother-in-law, John MacDonald of the Isles, becoming, in lowland opinion, a highland brigand and extorting protection money from the wealthy landowners and burgesses of Moray, which did not have a strong local leader. And so John of Fordun was inspired to paint the vehemently anti-highland picture mentioned above. Churchmen like Fordun liked peace and quiet and the royal Wolf and his merry men were upsetting order in a most unfamiliar way. But a word of warning. We get most of our information about Alexander from sources close to his brother, the second Robert (Fife/Albany), who was quickly consolidating his hold on power, having eased first his father and then his elder brother quietly out of the royal hot seat – not exactly an unbiased source!

Though the people of the north-east were certainly upset by this kind of activity, the vast majority of Scots were left to deal with more important issues. With the natural decrease in population already taking place by 1300, combined with the effects of repeated visitations of plague from the middle of the fourteenth century onwards, the balance of economic power now shifted away from those who owned land to those who could provide scarce labour. As general economic conditions began to pick up, it makes sense to suggest that some sections of society were able to better themselves. The nobility, watching falling land values with horror, doubtless tried to cling to past economic conditions. However, as was so often the case, the situation in Scotland doesn't seem to have been as extreme as, for example, in England, where legislation was passed to try to keep landlord incomes up and milk the growing wealth of the peasants. This led to a formidable, if ultimately unsuccessful, revolt by the latter in 1381.

Scottish trade was based, as it had been for thousands of years, on its basic raw materials – animal hides, timber, fish – as well as the more recently established low-grade cloth industry that was still capable of providing comparative wealth. The economy wasn't particularly sophisticated and Scottish urban communities were still tiny compared with elsewhere. Nevertheless the Scots had already established themselves with a staple port (one through which all their goods were channelled) in Bruges, centre of the European cloth industry (now in Belgium, then in the southern Netherlands). Scottish traders, both well-heeled merchants and small-scale packmen, were well-known in the Netherlands and around the Baltic, punching above their weight through sheer energy and dedication.

Robert III, who succeeded his father in 1390, perhaps does deserve his own epitaph as 'the worst of kings and most miserable of men'. But, yet again, it's difficult to trace the effects of a superficial weakening in central power on the wider community as the Stewarts began to tear themselves apart. The Scottish nobility, with notable exceptions like the earl of Douglas, largely left them to it.

Robert III also had little difficulty in producing sons, and eventually his eldest, David, began to challenge his uncle, Robert, duke of Albany, to be the power behind the throne. It was a tussle the young prince ultimately lost with his life, prompting the despairing king to send his next son to France for his 'education' in 1406. Disaster struck when English pirates boarded Prince James's boat and took him off for an English education instead. King Robert finally gave up on life completely, leaving his brother to continue as guardian of Scotland without the encumbrance of any near relatives.

Albany perhaps had to accommodate his fellow nobles more convincingly than a king, but it's hard to point to any real break with tradition in terms of overall crown-magnate relations and the way the country was run. Relations with England continued to be frosty/vaguely accommodating, depending on the circumstances, and we shouldn't forget that Albany's own son, Murdoch Stewart, also languished in England after yet another unsuccessful military attempt to regain Berwick in 1402.

Albany died in his eighties in 1420, and Murdoch, released from prison a few years previously, took over as guardian. Four years later he failed to prevent his cousin returning to reassert the active rights of the eldest branch of the family and the first James was crowned king of Scots. Within two years of his return, the Albany Stewarts had been destroyed (Murdoch himself was executed), bringing considerable lands, and therefore income, to King James. A plethora of legislation from parliaments held in the early years of the reign left no-one in any doubt that the new monarch meant business – things had, according to the king, been left to go to the dogs and he was the man to sort it out. Such an attitude was highly likely to put quite a few noble noses out of joint, since they had been getting on quite happily with the business of running the country without an active king for nearly forty years.

Fourteen years after his return from England, James I paid the ultimate price for increasing arbitrariness and the alienation of key members of the political community. But, yet again, it was members of his own extended family who were responsible for his assassination in 1437. The rest of the nobility were quite prepared to take him to task, refusing to follow him to a siege of Roxburgh (still held by the English) in 1436, but they would not sanction regicide. The dynasty, in the person of the next six-year-old King James, was secure.

James II is perhaps most remembered for the fiery birthmark on his face and his aggressive and controversial struggle to end the power of the Black Douglas family, both of which have been interpreted as evidence of a fairly violent temper. That may be true, but there was also an extremely practical reason for his Douglas fixation – the Crown's need for money in the face of falling customs returns. James II was the first Stewart king to make a glittering European marriage, in 1449, to Mary of Gueldres, niece of the duke of Burgundy. With her came an entrée into one of the richest courts in Europe and access to the latest high-tech artillery, but the downside was the major headache of trying to find enough money from royal lands in Scotland – now the most secure form of royal income – for her dower. It wasn't really James's fault: Europe had entered a recession and the wool trade was beginning to wind down permanently. Still, that doesn't exactly justify the destruction of a noble family, including the murder of one earl, William, in hot blood.

Having finally sent the Black Douglases into exile in England by 1455, James had to be very careful to treat the rest of his nobility with kid gloves. A number of new earls were created (including Argyll, originally Campbell of Lochawe) and a new honorific title – lord of parliament – was invented to reassure the magnates that their relationship with the king was as mutually-dependent as it had ever been. James continued to consult them regularly and his early demise in 1460 – killed by his own cannon at the siege of Roxburgh (still in English hands) – was genuinely shocking. However, yet again, the heir to the throne, a nine-year-old James, was crowned immediately.

These royal minorities could be seen as destabilizing. Historians in the past have certainly bemoaned the rise of particular noble families, gaining power and wealth through physical control of the young monarch during the minority. But, once again, we should wonder how much this affected the wider population and the answer these days seems to be not terribly much. Such minor imbalances also didn't last beyond the point at which the adult king took power fully upon himself.

James III, unlike his father in the last years of the reign at least, failed to understand some of the basic ground rules of Scottish *realpolitik*. But it would be unfair to accuse him of actually being any more high-handed or even vindictive than some of his namesakes. This James's problem was his PR. He preferred staying in Edinburgh (which now effectively

The remains of Roxburgh Castle, a fortress that changed hands between the English and the Scots for centuries. It was here that James II perished in 1460.

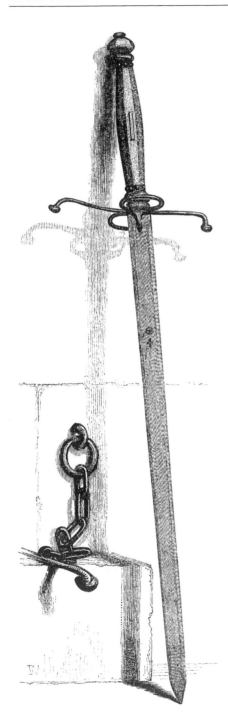

became the capital) in the company of his own friends rather than traipsing around the country, both listening to, and being heard by, his nobility – a key element of the personal lordship vested in a medieval monarch.

Like his father, James III also had to deal with the problem of a general trade recession and the limits to royal income that went with it. However, his response, of clipping the silver from the coinage and thereby devaluing it, met with stiff opposition, since the recession affected more pockets than just the king's. But James also failed to make any attempt to sweeten the policy for particular vested interests.

If an inability to see the need to interact with his wider political community lay at the root of James's unpopularity, he also suffered from an excess of another crucial element in the balance of power: near male relatives. James III was the first king since Robert III to have to contend with competition from family members. The most serious threat came from his younger brother, Alexander, duke of Albany, who set himself up first of all as the spokesman for the border nobility.

Despite the fall of the Black Douglases, the importance of the border as the first line of defence against England was still fundamental to Scottish politics. James III now challenged the whole outlook of these frontline nobles by seeking a rapprochement with the Auld Enemy. Albany clashed publicly with his brother over this issue, which seemed to strike at the very heart of the Scottish nation and its identity. It should not surprise us to learn that Blind Harry's *Wallace*, a vehemently anti-English epic poem about the great Scottish hero who never gave in to the English, was written at this time, the 1470s. One of the work's patrons, Sir Thomas Wallace of Craigie (of the senior branch of the Wallace family to which Sir William belonged), was exactly the kind of local mover and shaker who couldn't contemplate any lessening of the cold war.

This unusually large two-handed sword (5ft 9in in length) probably dates from the fifteenth century.

Craigie Castle, seat of the Wallace family. Sir Thomas Wallace was a relative of the famous William, a patron of Blind Harry and deeply anti-English.

However, James III's eventual obscure murder after an inconclusive battle against his own heir at Sauchieburn near Stirling in 1488 was, despite everything, far from a foregone conclusion. Though undoubtedly deeply unpopular, the king was only directly challenged by a few and most of the Scottish nobility remained strenuously neutral when it came to the final showdown. The instability of the first few years of James IV's reign indicates just how strongly the magnates abhorred the rocking of the political boat – by anyone. On the other hand, the fact that his brothers, step-uncles, wife and eldest sons all fell out badly with James III must lead us to conclude that this was a deeply difficult man who failed to maintain a stable balance of power at the centre, one of his main duties as king.

In the longer term, the most significant national event of James III's reign resulted from the king's marriage to Margaret, daughter of Christian I of Denmark, in 1469. Because her dowry payments (dowries are paid by fathers, dower by husbands) didn't materialize, Orkney and Shetland were confiscated three years later (Denmark had taken over Norway, which still owned the islands). Scotland as we know it had finally come into being.

In other aspects, Scotland thrived on stability. The royal burghs required protection from the crown to safeguard their trading privileges and parliament sometimes legislated to ensure that the crafts didn't upset the merchants too much. But the balance between these two elements of urban economic life – essentially lucrative overseas trade versus local manufacturing activity – varied from place to place and was rarely characterized by constant mutual antipathy.

In the countryside, the regulation of life continued to be the agricultural cycle itself, as well as the barony court, presided over by the local landowner. This fundamental legal institution dealt with the minutiae of agricultural activity, control of access to resources, such as timber – so necessary to Scottish rural life and work – and the administration of justice for most offences except the most serious without much reference to central government. Bonds of manrent, a formal agreement encouraging support and loyalty between a noble and a client effectively admitted that traditional 'feudal' ties of loyalty no longer worked and promoted relative stability in the localities. On the other hand, it placed a formidable amount of power in the hands of the landowners, in comparison with places like England and certainly Scandinavia, leaving most country folk at the mercy of the specific character and abilities of the local laird.

Medieval Scotland was certainly no model of peace and unity and violence was certainly not confined to the indulgent activities of the upper echelons of society. Borders society, for example, was based around a militarized way of life sanctioned by both governments as the most cost-effective method (from their point of view!) of maintaining the cold war that had characterized relations since the middle of the fourteenth century. But the borders was not the only part of Scotland which remained at arms length from central government, nor were the borderers alone in making a virtue and a way of life out of feuding.

The MacDonald lords of the Isles, who also became earls of Ross in 1437, had dominated the west highlands for well over a century by the beginning of James IV's reign. As already noted, they were not completely unwilling to play ball with the kings of Scots, but it helped if the man on the throne was interested in and accustomed to the politics of the north. Robert II had certainly fitted that bill, but from the acquisition of power by his brother Albany onwards the Crown remained firmly southern-orientated, viewing the highlands as a large amorphous problem. Direct action was rarely successful and may well have encouraged the highlanders to believe that they had little to fear from royal armies.

Interestingly, the highlands and the borders shared another feature in common: a vibrant literary culture (if its oral nature can be described as such). Poetry and songs particularly celebrated the martial exploits of a host of memorable characters but also reveal the sorrows and tragedies that inevitably accompanied the pitting of family against family in deadly enmity.

Having persuaded the nobility that he was truly sorry for his father's death, James IV spent the first decade of the reign attempting to 'daunt' the Isles. Perhaps he understood intuitively that a campaign against a perceived common enemy was a good way of promoting internal unity, though the policy probably created more unrest in the west than it solved.

James did manage to permanently forfeit the lordship of the Isles, thanks partly to treasonable dealings with the English by the MacDonalds in the previous reign and the

Knock Castle on Skye, constructed by the MacLeods in the fifteenth century, was one of countless fortifications in the Western Isles. It was taken over by the MacDonalds in the sixteenth century but was abandoned by 1689.

inability of the last lord, John, to control violent infighting within his family. However, it proved very difficult indeed to dismantle the power of the MacDonalds, despite the best efforts of other highland families, such as the Campbells of Argyll and MacKenzies of Kintail, who were keen to move into any potential power vacuum. The Crown probably pursued the worst kind of policy towards the area, punctuating long periods of total reliance on royal lieutenants like Argyll and the Gordon earl of Huntly, who tended to act in their own best interests, with feverish spells of direct action. It's no wonder that, in general, the highlands felt despised and put upon.

Like his father, James IV also made a significant marriage, to Margaret, daughter of Henry VII of England. Kings of Scots had married English princesses before – David II and James I in the more recent past. However, thanks to Henry VIII's well-publicized failure to produce a son, the Scottish crown found itself with an unusually personal interest in English dynastic matters as a result of this match. But that lay in the future. The main intention behind the marriage was the promotion of better Anglo-Scottish relations, though that was more Henry VII's vision than anyone else's.

James IV's reign is regarded as probably the most successful in Stewart history. And yet, it is now admitted, he was, if anything, even more high-handed and acquisitive than his father. The difference lay in the king's personality – James IV was as active, open and communicative as James III had been withdrawn. The reign is also renowned for its cultural achievements, though both James III and James V were also interested in architecture and the arts. James IV was responsible for the Great Hall at Stirling castle, restored to its former glory in 1999. The court, replicated throughout the land in the homes of the greater nobility,

In what was to prove an important dynastic match, James IV (above left, coin above) married Margaret Tudor (left), daughter of the English king Henry VII (below).

Norham Castle was besieged by James IV in 1513. After bombarding the walls with heavy artillery, James IV accepted the garrison's surrender before riding off to a fateful encounter at Flodden.

acted as a magnet for poets, minstrels, musicians, architects, scientists, painters and anyone else with an interesting take on life. In most aspects of art and architecture, thriving vernacular traditions were patronized alongside the very best from Europe. For a small country on the very edge of the continent, Scotland had nothing to be ashamed of.

Nevertheless, European politics could certainly prove a dangerous minefield and Stewart kings usually did best when they kept out of it. James IV, unfortunately, proved either unwilling or unable to avoid fulfilling his obligation to the French king, Louis XII, to invade England once Henry VIII had himself launched an attack on France. The battle of Flodden in 1513 was not the first or last occasion on which the Scots would find themselves short-changed by a Franco-Scottish alliance. However, the whole disastrous event surely brought serious questions about where Scotland's best interests were situated closer to the surface. And there's no doubt that the final irony of the reign lay in the fact that the king's own incredible popularity was directly responsible for the unprecedented numbers of his nobility who fought and died alongside him and the countless footsoldiers who always lost their lives in such events. The words of the old ballad, rewritten in the eighteenth century, touchingly sum up the heartbreak felt throughout the nation united in grief from the highest to the lowest.

> At e'en in the gloaming, nae swankies are roaming
> 'Bout stacks wi' the lasses at bogle to play [*hide and seek*]

> But each one sits drearie, lamenting her dearie, -
> The Flowers of the Forest are a' wede away. [*taken away*]
> > 'The Flowers of the Forest', Jean Elliot★

The reign of James IV was perhaps bathed in a more glorious retrospective light, not least because the loss of the king and the backbone of Scottish government and administration caused profound shock and even panic in the south particularly in the immediate aftermath of the battle. But, as ever, yet another child king was crowned and life went on – Scotland's political and administrative institutions were capable of coping even with this.

James V is sometimes overshadowed by his more scandalous daughter and the whole complicated issue of Scotland's conversion to Protestantism. Nevertheless, he left his mark on Scotland, particularly in the stunning architecture at Linlithgow and, most particularly, Stirling, which now boasted the first renaissance-style palace in Britain. His cultural influences, not to mention the cash to fund them, came partly from his marriages – political coups in themselves. His short-lived first wife was no less than a daughter of the French king, François, and his second was another Frenchwoman, the formidable Mary of Guise, who was also being courted by James's marriage-crazy uncle, Henry VIII.

Relations with England were far from easy, not least because Henry doesn't seem to have been the easiest monarch to get along with, either for his own subjects or European powers in general. But James, unlike his father, seems to have been fairly skilled at manipulating the increasingly complex and religious-orientated politics of Europe to his own ends. Hence his success in the marriage game as François of France sought to keep England and Scotland apart.

But his greatest coup was the financial inducements that he extracted from the pope to keep him firmly Catholic, especially after Henry VIII turned Protestant, having failed to get a divorce from the pope in 1533. Given *carte blanche* to exercise patronage over the Scottish church, the king took his predecessors' ability to milk cash from the kirk to a new extreme. The irony of James V's reign was that his very financial success pushed the church into feuing their lands, which, as we will see, was extremely unpopular. This in turn helped to fuel the flames of Protestantism, something that James himself had no interest in.

Feu-farming (implying a money rent) was not a new form of land tenure: there are many references to it in the thirteenth century, for example. But the wars with England had placed renewed emphasis on the need to retain military service in return for land and the practice had gone out of fashion. However, as the need for hard cash to pay for the luxuries and necessities of elite living increased, particularly during a time of recession, the system began to make more sense. Basically, a tenant would now pay an increased rent and a grassum, or lump sum, when he entered or inherited the property, and in return he owned it forever. For any landowner requiring extra cash quickly – such as the Scottish kirk faced with heavy and increasingly regular tax bills from the king – it was a marvellous

★ *Songs of Scotland*, ed. Wilma Paterson, Edinburgh, 1996

quick fix. The only thing they hadn't reckoned with was inflation, stemming largely from a debasement of the coinage, combined with population growth outstripping food supply. Although the rents were increased when the land was first feued, they couldn't be raised thereafter.

The advantages to the tenant are fairly obvious too – now a man could plan ahead, secure in the knowledge that, so long as the rent could be paid, the property would remain in his family forever. But for many others, these changes were a disaster, because they simply could not afford the initial increases and were forced off their land. So some did rather well, beginning to rise above their social equals, while others faced economic and social ignominy. The church, which presided over the most wholesale and precipitate process of feu-farming, got the blame, though the real culprit, and beneficiary, was the king.

James V, like his father, comes across as a confident European monarch, albeit of a small northern kingdom. His court was the usual mixture of the great, the good and the exotic. The king loved to hunt, a typical royal – not to mention Stewart – pastime. He also had a

James V was another successful king, succeeding in bolstering the royal finances while at the same time building palaces and enjoying the ostentatious consumption expected of a sixteenth-century European ruler.

keen sense of his own importance in the world, commissioning the pre-eminent symbol of royal power in its most exalted guise – the closed imperial crown – to be displayed in stone in the courtyard at Linlithgow and on the very spire of Edinburgh's kirk, St Giles.

But for all his determination to be admired, we also see something of the humanity of this James and the people of his court. As the 'guid man' of Ballengeich (an area of Stirling), he had a reputation for wandering around the town incognito, mixing with his lesser subjects and enjoying their leisure activities of drinking and story-telling. He may even stare down at us as a gargoyle on his new palace at Stirling, while the lords and ladies of his court take their places on the walls inside, immortalized as some of the models for the famous Stirling heads still to be seen in the castle. For all his unpleasantness and avarice, this was still a king who could listen and learn from Sir David Lindsay's telling and hilarious morality play *The Three Estates* (referring to the component parts of the Scottish parliament), a satire on the state of Scotland's government that reaches across the centuries even into our own times.

But, for all the energy and seeming modernity of the reign, the end of it came in very similar circumstances to that of his father. Relations with England finally broke down in 1541 and another invasion across the border was planned. Yet again the Scots found themselves on the receiving end of an English bludgeoning, this time at Solway Moss near Gretna in November 1542. The king wasn't even present, but retired immediately afterwards to his favourite hunting lodge at Falkland in Fife where he died of a mixture of extreme Stewart angst and heartbreak at his own inability to beget sons. But he did have an heir: his one-week-old daughter, Mary. For the first time since the 1280s, Scotland faced the prospect of a woman on the throne, with all the accompanying problems that went with such an eventuality in a world dominated by men.

The Scotlands of 1357 and 1542 differed more in style than substance. Power was still highly uncentralized and kingship continued to rely on the traditional relationship between centre and localities, as well as on the personal managerial knack of the individual monarchs. Despite individual failures in that crucial role, the dynasty itself remained resolutely inviolate, certainly in comparison to elsewhere in Europe and most particularly Scotland's southern neighbour, which had swapped royal lines on no less than two occasions in that period.

On the other hand, nothing stays the same forever, especially in politics, not even the machinery of government. By 1541 central government had increased the extent of its rights – and responsibilities – considerably. In 1532, thanks to church taxation, a college of justice was established in Edinburgh, providing the nation with a fixed central lawcourt for the first time. And speaking of taxation, the regularity with which contributions were now demanded makes something of a mockery of the established notion that Scotland remained a tax-free haven except in exceptional circumstances.

Underpinning all this, the fundamental resource base and the agricultural grind that defined the lives of the vast majority of western European people continued unchanged in any significant aspect. Each inhabitant of each community that, ultimately, added up to Scotland lived out his or her lives with only perhaps the most salacious interest in what

Henry VIII, whose army dealt a severe blow to the Scots at Flodden in 1513 and Solway Moss in 1542.

was going on in the lives of the royal family. However, it was a different kettle of fish if the court actually happened to be in residence in the area, giving a boost to the local economy, underlining the symbiotic nature of the relationship between crown and people, and perhaps bringing a sense of pride and unity to those who might otherwise maintain a distinctly ambivalent attitude to the whole business. Of course, the Stewart kings took the whole issue of their royalty seriously, but, on balance, they perhaps didn't take it all *too* seriously.

Though the overwhelming majority lived on the land, the tiny Scottish burghs played a significant role, well above their numeric strength (both as a group and in terms of the proportion of the population who lived there), in the nation's economic wellbeing. Thanks to the general recession, a comparative tightening of belts had been necessary in the fifteenth century but exports eventually began to increase again from the 1530s onwards. However, the biggest change since the golden days of the thirteenth century was not the drop in wealth from the wool trade but the rise of Edinburgh as Scotland's pre-eminent burgh out of the vacuum left by Berwick. The major trading ports were clustered on the east coast, for the obvious reason that Scotland's trading partners, with the exception of England, were all across on the European mainland to the east – it would be many centuries before Glasgow began to figure significantly as an urban centre.

As today, the urban environment housed extremes of wealth and poverty, usually living in fairly close proximity to each other. The east coast ports, a literal haven for boats from all over Europe, bore most of the terrible burden of the recurrences of plague and there was little, particularly in terms of standards of hygiene, to prevent each outbreak from cutting a swathe through their citizens at will.

But disease wasn't the only factor affecting the urban population. The meteoric rise of Edinburgh, which had cornered 60% of Scotland's export market by 1500, had a huge effect on the distribution of trading activity in the east. Some communities, like the small villages of Fife and the Lothian coast, could make the most of an evolving situation, acting as service points for commodities such as salt that were required to serve Edinburgh's growing needs, though their heyday would not come for another hundred years. Others, particularly Aberdeen, were sufficiently geographically removed and endowed with a large enough hinterland of their own to carve out their own niche. But the rest found it difficult to make much headway.

So, the squeeze that the capital's pre-eminence put on the opportunities available to most of the other Scottish burghs kept them relatively small – only Edinburgh, Aberdeen, Dundee and Perth boasted a population of more than 5,000 in early modern Scotland, and the rest of the top sixty burghs could claim less (often far less) than 3,000 citizens. On the other hand, the lack of population pressure usually (though not absolutely) meant that social tensions were also kept to a minimum, despite the terrible hardships experienced by the urban poor. Nevertheless, it's very hard for modern western Europeans to envisage just how much of a strain on the senses, not to mention the nervous system, life in a medieval town, even a small Scottish one, must have been. Those who were used to it probably stopped noticing the stench of humans and animals, but visitors from the countryside probably dreaded having to come in to town.

The Scottish nobility also hadn't had an easy time of it in economic terms, having watched their incomes drop dramatically since 1300, most notably in relation to the value of land. As already mentioned, the constant revisitations of plagues is presumed to have kept the overall population down (the evidence is not terribly forthcoming), so there was to be no immediate remedy through a reversal of the basic economic balance between land and labour. There was no such thing as a typical Scottish noble, and each family reacted differently to changing conditions according to the individuals in charge and the resources and opportunities available. However, as the sixteenth century progressed, one significant development appears to have been the frequency and extent of noble indebtedness: keeping up with Lord Jones in increasing conspicuous consumption was not necessarily restricted by the amount of hard cash available, but ultimately there was a price to be paid.

1. A Scottish orchid. Scotland's flora and fauna is still remarkable in places, but it is nowhere near as diverse as it was many thousands of years ago.

2. Scotland currently has around 15% of its land surface under trees, including modern plantations. Fragments of Scotland's ancient semi-natural woods can still be found, but they are all profoundly influenced by past management regimes.

3. Scotland's great mountain wildernesses are very popular today as tourist destinations, but in the past they have usually housed human populations, field systems, some forestry and small-scale industrial concerns, as well as animal grazing areas.

4. *The people of Skara Brae gave great consideration to the environment they lived in when constructing their settlement. They also respected the need of each family to maintain some privacy, despite living closely together.*

5. *Prehistoric villages generally made the most of whatever was to hand as building materials – rushes, heather, timber, soil. The insides of houses were very dark, though quite cosy – an ideal breeding ground for extra guests in the form of flies.*

6. *The Ring of Brodgar, like other stone circles, was intended to be seen from a distance. The construction of these massive ritual spaces involved a considerable effort on the part of the community involved. However, whether or not everyone was permitted inside these sacred areas, it seems most likely that tribal leadership devolved on experienced members of the group rather than being located at the top of a defined hierarchy.*

7. *The Broch of Gurness is also meant to be seen from a distance, as well to dominate access from the sea to this part of Orkney. Brochs did most probably house noble families who lived separately from those lower down the social order. However, the village pictured here surrounding the broch was built over five hundred years later when the whole area had become part of Pictland.*

8. *Dundurn, a hill fort in Strathearn, is situated in a narrow glen whose western end is bounded by Loch Earn. The invading Dal Riatans made their way into Pictland along this route (among others), hence the need for a hill fort to try to stem their progress. Not that it worked!*

9. *The iconography of Pictish stones is still a great mystery. Depictions of actual events or people sit alongside other fantastical creatures, like this mermaid or sea monster*

10. *Crossraguel abbey was founded in the thirteenth century by Duncan, earl of Carrick, in whose earldom it was situated. It was a daughter house of Paisley Abbey, whose patrons were the Stewarts. Crossraguel suffered greatly during the wars of independence and, sadly, its charters have not survived in great numbers to help us piece together its history and that of the surrounding area.*

11. *Inchcolm Abbey in the Firth of Forth was established in the twelfth century. Its most famous abbot was Walter Bower, who wrote his* Scotichronicon – *chronicle of the Scots – in the fifteenth century.*

12. *Soutra, south of Edinburgh, is an unusual example of the remains of a medieval hospital. It has survived primarily because, though it used to sit on the main road between Scotland and England, we now travel up and down other routes. Edward I stayed here on his way north into Scotland on campaign.*

13. *Duffus castle near Elgin is a classic motte and bailey castle. It was built for the Anglo-Norman family of de Freskin, who were given lands in Scotland by David I in the twelfth century. Their job was to police the area for the Crown, given that Moray, the area in which the castle is situated, was still uneasy about accepting Scottish royal authority.*

14. *Caerlaverock castle on the Solway near Dumfries is a most elegant, shield-like construction. Henry III took exception to it when it was built in the mid-thirteenth century since he viewed it as an offensive action on the part of the Scots, so close to the border.*

15. Berwick became the headquarters of the English occupation of Scotland after 1296 (though it sometimes moved back into Scottish hands). John Balliol was pronounced king in the great hall here, a job which he may have wondered why he had bothered appying for. Berwick's status as Scotland's premier burgh was effectively ruined by the wars and the decline in the European wool trade in the later middle ages.

16. Castle Gloom (now Castle Campbell), east of Stirling was a seat of the earls, later dukes, of Argyll. Given that they were so influential at court, they needed a country seat near to Edinburgh (where they also had a house). Despite the name, the castle is very pleasantly situated and designed for elegant living. It is regularly used for weddings today.

17. Glencoe, scene of the famous massacre. The MacDonalds of Glencoe were not alone in failing to take the oath of allegiance to King William, rather than the exiled King James, in time. However, they were notorious cattle thieves and lived in this bottle-shaped glen, making them the perfect target for teaching recalcitrant highland clans a lesson. The whole unhappy event backfired completely on the government and outraged even lowland opinion which was generally not terribly sympathetic to the highlands.

18. Ruthven barracks, en route to Inverness from Perth, were built as part of the government's attempt to control the highlands in the aftermath of the rebellion of 1715. Ironically, Ruthven served as a rallying point for Jacobites after their defeat at Culloden in 1746, but Bonnie Prince Charlie was already making his way back to the continent. The Jacobite rebellions were over.

19 & 20. The House of Dun was built in 1730 for David Erskine, Lord Dun, a prominent Jacobite. It is a fine example of eighteenth-century architecture and contains some exquisite wall decoration which overtly incorporates Jacobite symbolism. Note the poor Scottish lion in the bottom of the picture squashed under the weight of British imperialism.

21. The Discovery, *the vessel which carried Captain Scott on his fateful expedition to the Antarctic. These solid wooden boats had already seen impressive service in the Arctic as whaling ships. Dundee, where the* Discovery *now resides, was the Scottish capital of this industry.*

22. *A scene from Scott's final Antarctic expedition of 1912, with the* Discovery *ice-bound in the background. A brave attempt to be first to the South Pole, the venture ended in disaster – the explorers perished and the Norwegian Roald Amundsen took the coveted title.*

23. *The Wallace Monument, near Stirling, was constructed at the end of the nineteenth century by a group of predominantly pro-Unionist prominent Scots after a public subscription scheme had raised the funds. Stirling and the surrounding area might be regarded as a Scottish Belgium considering the number of battles that have been fought in the vicinity.*

24. *Scotland's shipbuilding industry, associated predominantly with Clydeside, was world-class. Its slow and painful demise, along with other great manufacturing industries, caused the nation to lack confidence throughout much of the twentieth century. However, the contraction of the British empire's economic capacity was not Scotland's fault. Here, the Mauretania steams under the Forth Bridge on her way to be broken up at Rosyth, north of Edinburgh. The masts of the giant ship had to be cut to allow her to pass under the famous bridge.*

25. *Improvement led to the amalgamation of the smaller farmtouns into single farms. Fields became larger. However, the twentieth century also witnessed a new era of commercial plantation forestry. Here we can see the impact of these modern ideas on the Scottish landscape. The multi-purpose landuse systems which existed for thousands of years have been destroyed, condemned as inefficient and unproductive. However, we may be changing our minds on that issue and going back, on a small scale, to a system which allows animals and trees to grow together under careful supervision, for example.*

Scalloway Castle, Shetland, was one of many new castles of the sixteenth century.

And there *were* tactics that could improve a noble's lot. Taking advantage of power vacuums, as happened in the borders with the expulsion of the Douglases and in the west highlands after the forfeiture of the lordship of the Isles, was one tried and tested method. Loyal royal service often worked a treat, except, as the Douglases again exemplify, if your wealth prompted even the Crown to cast envious eyes in your direction. However, playing power games during a royal minority rarely did anyone any good in the long run, unless you were already extremely powerful.

But perhaps the greatest enemy was Mother Nature herself, as manifested in the inevitable eventual failure of male lines in every family. The Stewarts were actually incredibly fortunate to last from 1371 to 1542 without coming up against the possibility of a female succession. Indeed, the main problem seems to have been a surfeit of males on a number of occasions. But such biological inevitabilities, combined with manmade contributions such as the unprecedented number of aristocratic fatalities at Flodden and the need for hostages for the royal ransoms of David II and James I, could wreak havoc on the number of adult noblemen available for governmental service. It's just as well the churchmen were still more than happy to administer the law and man the civil service.

By 1542 the Scottish church had acquired not just one but two archbishops (St Andrews and Glasgow), finally achieving the direct hierarchical link between the state and the papacy that had eluded it for centuries. Coincidentally, this also made it rather more difficult for the English church to argue that the Scottish church was subordinate to it.

Individual churchmen continued to make their mark in government, proving indispensable, as ever, to their royal masters, whom they managed to serve with relative ease alongside their papal one. As a result of a number of schisms in the fifteenth century, when Europe ended up with three popes and a church council had to sort the whole issue out, the vexed question of where ultimate authority within western Christendom actually lay proved difficult for popes to ignore in practice, whatever the official view. This, together with the weight of theological questioning that tempted many a devoted Catholic into the sin of error, provided the increasingly articulate and confident European laity with far too much food for thought. The way in which the papacy dealt with what it perceived as attacks on its monopoly of truth – but which were far often merely the results of intellectual inquisitiveness – was to be crucial to the history of the religious upheavals of the sixteenth century.

However, we should not make the mistake of presuming that Catholicism was in itself decaying and moribund, riven with corruption and ripe for the new broom of the Protestant movement. Many of the issues that taxed the faithful were not new and there was a clear dedication to genuine reform that found itself reflected in equally genuine examples of continuing traditional piety. And, as has already been pointed out, the issue that caused the most genuine concern and downright hostility – the feuing of church lands – was a strategy forced on the Scottish kirk, caught between the papal need to keep individual kings safe and Catholic and the intemperate royal demands for cash that followed.

It is also important to point out that despite the nepotism that made important church offices such as the archbishopric of St Andrews a haven for illegitimate royal offspring, many Scottish churchmen, including controversial incumbents, proved worthy occupants of their positions. When discussing the transformation of Scotland into an ostensibly Protestant nation, it is vitally important that we should not regard the issue as a foregone conclusion. James V, for one, would surely have been extremely shocked by the turn of events that led to the Reformation of 1560, a mere eighteen years after his death. If there is one thing that the history of Scotland so far would seem to indicate, it is that the road to radical change was something of a contradiction in terms. A faint and meandering sheep track would seem to be more appropriate.

EIGHT

Reformation to Revolution
1542 – 1702

As with the wars of independence, it's hard to imagine Scottish history without the Reformation. And yet, if anything, Scotland's history up until then suggested that the nation would continue to follow a French, not an English, line in making its mind up over the question of religion. In that case, Scotland should have stayed Catholic, since that remained the official policy in France, despite a bitter civil war over religious issues. This is not meant to imply that power politics and foreign relations alone dictated the issue. Questions of personal religious preference were obviously vitally important. But revolutions tend to happen when the private desires of the individual, or some individuals, coincide with the larger dynamics of power and privilege. If a straw poll had been conducted in the 1550s it's seriously to be doubted if a majority in Scotland would have voted for fundamental change in the current religious status quo, however much reform was seen as desirable at most levels. Major change was not something that Scotland had proved terribly keen on up until 1560.

Religion, in this period, cut across the boundaries of economic, social, cultural and political, as well as spiritual, life. The church obviously continued to work hard on its fundamental role in the care of souls. But let's not forget that kirk and crown had collaborated for hundreds of years in running the country, whether in foreign policy, the mechanisms of government and administration, matters of education or the law.

Much of the problem, as mentioned in Chapter Seven, lay with the papacy's own reaction to religious dissent, which it discouraged. But as the sixteenth century progressed, there was a limit to the extent to which the church's guardians of orthodoxy could stem a widening theological debate, as well as criticism of the way it conducted its affairs. We shouldn't forget that Scotland's first university, St Andrews, was founded explicitly in 1413 to promote such orthodoxy, but, ironically, in the sixteenth century its own students were often at the forefront of the honourable business of challenging their tutors, who were still all churchmen. This could be seriously damaging to student health, and a number of them were burned for their views.

One of the most crucial issues of the day was who had access to the word of God. This became a critical issue for the church with the advent of printing, which arrived in Scotland in 1508. This incredible new technology revolutionised society's intellectual experience by widening the opportunity to actually read texts far beyond the select few who might be able to put their hands on a manuscript. Once copies of William Tyndale's translation of the bible into English became available in the 1530s, the Church's domination of doctrinal truth looked extremely shaky.. It's now hard to imagine a black market in religious texts, with copies being sneaked around in an under-the-counter/brown paper bag kind of a way. Perhaps at the back of people's minds was the notion that the church perhaps had something to hide; at the very least one should be allowed to check for oneself.

The Church, on the other hand, argued that it required a considerable amount of training before this powerful knowledge could be handed over, including skills in reading

William Tyndale, whose translation of the bible into English caused outrage in the Church.

the languages of the originals. And it did take its role in education seriously, encouraging the laity in general to become more literate with the 1494 Education Act, which stated that the eldest sons of lairds should all receive a basic grounding in reading and writing. Unfortunately, the counter argument could be presented with one dismissive sweep of the hand towards some of the parish priests, who, it was alleged, were often unable to even read and write, never mind get to grips with the classics. Yet they were supposed to be viewed as the unquestionable moral authority in each parish.

As more and more Scots took advantage of this encouragement towards literacy, the Church's monopoly of knowledge, and therefore of truth, began to seriously disintegrate. In Scotland, as elsewhere, orthodoxy was promoted as much by the Crown as by the Church itself – neither institution was very keen on dissent. But, increasingly, many sections of society began to feel alienated by perceived anomalies – anomalies that had often always been there but which hadn't, until now, assumed such importance.

The issue of the church's wealth was clearly a crucial one, especially with the particularly Scottish issue of feu-farming in the background. Much of the ire of those who found it difficult to square the church of Christ's ministry with the vast multinational corporation of the later middle ages was directed at the friars. Explicitly charged with the task of preaching to the faithful to combat new ideas, they were not necessarily the worst offenders, but were certainly the most visible and active since they tended to operate in centres of population rather than living cloistered in monasteries in the countryside. Within that urban context, also, the friars perhaps stood out as a distinctive and wealthy group outside the control of the burgh elites.

The merchants, who formed the backbone of urban wealth, were extremely influential in issues related to personal devotion and religious experience, even though they were not usually directly involved in either educational or national governmental processes. Many spent much of their working lives in Europe, exercising their entrepreneurial skills and discussing matters of common interest with their colleagues across the continent. These men were used to making decisions for themselves, to controlling their own destinies. Once they had heard the new ideas, it was difficult to just forget them again, especially if they agreed with them.

But a complex web had to mesh together before Scotland could contemplate the real possibility of denying the authority of the pope and accepting the major doctrinal shift towards Protestantism, and it was by no means predetermined. Protestantism offered a number of important benefits to the movers and shakers in early modern Scotland, just as the Christian religion had once sold itself to the leaders of early Scottish society. The direct relationship with God, with no priest acting as intermediary, was perhaps a major attraction for many of those who were used to dictating the shape of their lives here on earth. And then there was the increasingly difficult political situation that Scotland found itself in during the 1540s and '50s.

The death of James V, leaving only a tiny princess as his heir, placed Scotland in an unaccustomed constitutional position. There wasn't much point in looking around the major powers of western Europe for precedents either, since kingdoms such as England

and France usually worked very hard to avoid the possibility of the succession of a queen. Spain, a very recent creation, had managed to cope with a joint monarch when Queen Isabella of Castile joined personal and political forces with Ferdinand of Aragon in the fifteenth centur, and Queen Margaret of Denmark was a huge success in her own right. But that was about it.

The caretaker governments of under-age monarchs were often (though not always) responsible for arranging the marriages of their royal charges, which could bring important advantages to the crown in particular, but also the country in general. The choice of the future husband of Mary Queen of Scots was a matter of fundamental state importance since it was assumed that the prospective partner, while obviously necessary for the production of an heir, would exert unusual power by definition of their respective genders.

Henry VIII was well aware of the political and constitutional implications of Scotland's current situation. And so was the French king, François I. The danger for each of the great powers of Europe lay in the possibility of the little queen marrying the son of either of them, and thereby placing Scotland irretrievably in one camp or the other. To begin with, Henry looked to have taken the initiative successfully, reaping the benefits of a longer-term strategy, begun during the minority of James V, of encouraging the growth of a pro-English party within Scottish politics.

In the initial aftermath of James's death, two of the key Catholic figures of subsequent years of the minority, the queen-dowager, Mary of Guise-Lorraine, and Cardinal Beaton, were not yet fully established politically. Henry continued to cultivate pro-English sympathizers among the Scottish nobility, including the heir-presumptive, James Hamilton, earl of Arran. In March 1543 Arran was appointed as Governor of the kingdom and this smoothed the way to a marriage treaty of the same year which would have seen Henry VIII's son, Edward, marry Mary. But Arran, who ultimately wanted to be king, overplayed his hand and was forced to admit important members of the pro-Catholic, pro-French party, such as Beaton, into government.

Henry reacted with considerable fury to the emergence of an overtly anti-English policy in Scotland, launching the euphemistically named 'Rough Wooing' (so-called because the campaigns were aimed at securing the marriage of the little queen) on his northern neighbour. But such aggressive tactics didn't exactly endear his cause to the Scots, and helped his enemies in Scotland to portray the French as the kingdom's protectors. In the meantime, Cardinal Beaton instigated a programme of reform through a number of provincial councils, resulting eventually in the authorization of a catechism in Scots and increasing use of preaching as a means of engaging with the faithful.

The English government continued to encourage Scottish Protestants to try to take the initiative in the north. However, the murder of Cardinal Beaton and seizure of St Andrews castle in 1546 by a group which included John Knox was left seriously in the lurch by English forces whose headquarters were only across the Forth in Haddington. French troops were also now directly involved, successfully besieging St Andrews in 1547. The 'Rough Wooing' continued even after the death of Henry VIII in that year but in 1548 Mary Queen of Scots was finally packed off, out of harm's way, to France.

The Queen Dowager Mary of Guise, who assumed an important role following the death of her husband, James V.

It was quite flattering, in a way, that both England and France should be fighting over Scotland. But it was the kind of attention Scotland could do without. With Beaton dead and Arran, the regent, most concerned to do nothing to jeopardize his own royal ambitions, the stage was set for the emergence of a new political figure in Scotland, Mary of Guise-Lorraine.

Though she did not become regent officially until 1554, the Queen Dowager had played a key role in Scottish politics for at least a decade. Naturally pro-French and Catholic, her first concern was nevertheless to secure the stability of the kingdom for her daughter. However, by 1558, the year in which Mary Queen of Scots finally married the dauphin, François, tensions were high. Insecurity was rife throughout the kingdom, exacerbated by (correct) rumours that the marriage treaty gave Mary's husband the right to rule Scotland as king should she die before him. Scotland was facing the very real prospect of annexation by France.

In the years leading up to her death in 1560, the Queen Regent did her best to reassure as many vested interests as was both possible and wise given her fundamental policy.

John Knox, the radical reformer of the Scottish Church.

Protestant sympathizers continued to operate covertly within Scotland but as late as 1559 their support was extremely limited. In May of that year John Knox preached the kind of fire-raising sermon for which he was renowned in Perth, provoking a riot in that volatile burgh. But such actions could be as counter-productive as they were dramatic: for the Protestant nobility, social unrest was not something to be encouraged.

However, increasing fears about French domination played into the hands of the Lords of the Congregation, as the Protestant nobility were known. Their appeal, from October 1559 onwards, was to patriotism, across the board of individual religious conviction. The Queen Regent was deposed at the same time and Arran, now firmly Protestant again, resumed his former role, though Mary of Guise-Lorraine was far from a spent political force. By January 1560, an English fleet had arrived to help remove French garrisons and in February the first non-marriage treaty of mutual aid between Scotland and England, now ruled by Elizabeth, was concluded at Berwick.

For these few months the issue would seem to have been far more political than religious, though obviously the two were interlinked. A *coup d'état* had taken place, though, as ever in Scotland, not against the dynasty itself. Nevertheless, religious reform was very much on the agenda and in March 1560 parliament met with dubious legality. An official move towards Protestantism was the price of the support of a key number of localities – Angus and the Mearns, Fife, Lothian and Ayrshire. It was well attended and not just by the

Protestants. Though we don't know the details of the debate, which must surely have been 'interesting' to say the least, its outcome was far more certain: the abolition of the mass, a denial of the pope's authority and acceptance of a Protestant Confession of Faith. The only snag lay in the fact that, to become law, these acts ultimately required the Queen to ratify them.

This religious revolution was not quite over yet. It required a blueprint which duly appeared in the following year as *The First Book of Discipline*. Unfortunately the vision of a new Protestant Scottish utopia was severely undermined by the nobility's reticence to hand over much of the Catholic church's revenues to fund it. Equally problematic was the obvious lack of Protestant personnel to man the new church, though the fact that many of those already in position converted to the new religion made life both simpler and more complicated. A degree of continuity surely made these huge changes more palatable in areas of the country that had little or no history of Protestant affinity. On the other hand, the neat, sensible administrative set-up envisaged by the *Book of Discipline* was soon diluted by the need for pragmatic accommodation with existing structures.

Though we can certainly question the extent to which Protestantism took root in every parish throughout Scotland for many decades after the Reformation, the events of 1559-1560 were still remarkable. And the transition to Protestantism had been achieved with a minimum of violence. But then, History made an unexpected throw of the dice and the recently widowed nineteen-year-old Queen decided to come home to Scotland.

It iss difficult to deal with the personal reign of Mary Queen of Scots sensibly, as with any iconic and deeply emotive subject in Scottish history. Even current historians are deeply divided in their attitudes towards her. In part, she suffers from a) being beautiful (not a condition always to inspire rationality) b) being a female monarch in a deeply conservative, chauvinistic kingdom like Scotland, and c) being on the throne at the same time as Elizabeth I of England, who proved that masculine attributes and effective sovereignty could be housed within the frail body of a woman.

Nevertheless, for the first five years after her return Mary managed to steer a fairly successful course through Scottish politics, predominantly by keeping well out of it. She did nothing to upset the status quo as established in 1560, apart from not actually ratifying the acts of the Reformation parliament. Like her grandfather, James IV, she toured the country energetically, providing many a castle with the lucrative claim that she slept there. Like her predecessors, also, she presided over a dazzling court that encouraged the very best in poetry and music and provided the nobility – Protestant or Catholic – with the usual milieu in which to play for favour and patronage.

The question of her marriage dominated these early years and was of great interest, as when she was a baby, to the powers of continental Europe, as well as her cousin Elizabeth. In the end, she settled for an internal candidate and distant relative, Henry Stewart, Lord Darnley, who was both Catholic and, like Arran, a contender for her throne. To be fair, whatever the queen did would have appalled someone and Elizabeth's solution, to stay unmarried and therefore childless, was not really an option, especially for someone who viewed herself and her descendants as the next monarchs of England.

Clockwise from above: Mary Queen of Scots, to this day the nation's greatest romantic heroine; Henry Lord Darnley, her first husband (painted with his younger brother); the earl of Bothwell, widely regarded as Darnley's murderer; Loch Leven Castle, where Mary was imprisoned before her flight to England.

The jury will never provide a unanimous verdict on Mary Queen of Scots. Her forced abdication in 1567 was the result, ostensibly, of her liaison with James Hepburn, earl of Bothwell, a man strongly implicated in the murder of Darnley in 1566. But perhaps bigger issues were at stake, including the upbringing of her infant son, James, who had been baptized a Catholic in 1566. Her abdication was not, of course, the end of the story. Even her flight to England in 1568 failed to stem the bitterness of a civil war that dragged on until 1573.

However, the abdication of 1567 was significant in a number of ways. In the first place, the elaborate theories put forward to justify what was in effect a palace revolution made absolutely explicit previous ideas about the relationship between the monarch and his/her people. Previous monastic writers, such as the author of the chronicle *The Book of Pluscarden* had commented on the responsibilities of the Crown to the people and the nation, even hinting that removing a monarch could be justifiable if he looked likely to damage Scotland's interests. However, George Buchanan, leader of the Scottish kirk in 1567 and later tutor to the young James VI, reflected at length on the contractual nature of kingship, with the balance of power, according to him, lying with the political community which regulated the monarch's behaviour. His former pupil by no means agreed with him once he had grown up.

Secondly, the removal of a Catholic monarch from the head of a Protestant realm not only paved the way for the 'proper' education of the heir to the throne, but also enabled a much more fundamental Protestant revolution to take place. Intrinsic to this second, more Calvinist, reformation was the development of the view that presbyterianism, which placed church government in the hands of officials chosen from among the godly on an equal footing, was infinitely preferable to the current hierarchical system of

James Stewart (left), earl of Moray and half-brother of Mary Queen of Scots, acted as regent for the young James VI. A prominent Protestant during his sister's reign, Moray formed part of the Protestant circle surrounding the young king and was influential in the appointment of George Buchanan as the young king's tutor.

bishops and archbishops. Such a system would also effectively break the fundamental link between Church and State that had existed since Christianity first came to Scotland. It was little wonder, therefore, that such views met with little favour among the Stewart monarchs.

During the queen's last years of tedious imprisonment in England, perhaps not even she believed that there was any real chance of her restoration. Her unwilling hostess, Elizabeth, torn between the real danger of the presence of this Catholic potential heir-presumptive to her throne and her natural abhorrence of any challenge to the rights of a lawfully anointed monarch, however politically awkward, finally signed the death warrant. In February 1587 Mary, Queen of Scots was executed, ending years of frustration and embarrassment for herself, Elizabeth and her son, not to mention Scotland itself. In her end was the beginning of something much bigger and enduring: her legend.

So how was Scotland different in the decades after 1560? In many fundamental ways, it had not changed at all. Wealth and land may have been removed from particular ecclesiastical control (though revenues were already being diverted into the pockets of the crown and the nobility long before 1560), but it certainly wasn't being redistributed around society as a whole. One of the main changes was the interest in, and punishment of, a whole raft of misdemeanours, the most obvious of which was being Catholic but which also encompassed sexual misconduct. This was only possible because the state as a whole, from parliament down to the burgh magistrates, was willing to co-operate in this fairly prurient attention to everyone else's business. Of course, it usually depended who you were as to whether or not you were hauled up in front of the kirk's authorities and forced to make public penance for immoral behaviour.

This more Old Testament view of the relationship between behaviour and punishment on this earth also helps to explain, in part, the growth of another phenomenon that sprang up in the post-Reformation period in both Catholic and Protestant countries: the execution of witches. Anyone who has seen Arthur Miller's *The Crucible* will be well aware of the fine line between private vendetta and public hysteria and the relationship between economic jealousy or difficulty and attacks on those for whom their neighbours had reasons for dislike that had nothing to do with the supernatural. Women accounted for the overwhelming majority of those tried and punished for dealings with the devil, reflecting society's deep-seated fear of the female, particularly those whose activities fell beyond properly accepted norms, including dependence on men. On the other hand, as James VI's own ventures into print on the subject made clear, the extirpation of witchcraft fitted neatly into an intellectual framework that believed that the activities of individuals within society impinged directly on the health and wellbeing of the state as a whole.

Throughout Europe, there seems to have been some correlation between an upsurge in witch-hunting activity and periods of economic difficulty, but this was far from the whole story, certainly in Scotland. Despite the modern equation of extreme Protestantism, particularly Calvinism, with the encouragement of individualist economic principles, Scotland's economic outlook also remained noticeably unaffected by the religious upheaval. The individual pursuit of wealth as a godly practice – in essence, the free market

A 'Witch's Bridle' from Forfar. The cruel headpiece, which prevented speech, was worn by condemned witches on their way to the stake.

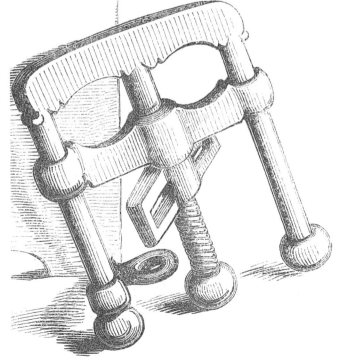

A small set of thumb-screws once used for eliciting confessions in the burgh of Montrose.

141

economy - was still a long way off and protectionist legislation continued to give the royal burghs in particular considerable advantages over competitors.

On the other hand, conspicuous consumption among the nobility and expanding lairdly class was a definite feature of the later sixteenth century. Rents were still paid partly in kind (i.e. in labour service or agricultural produce) but money rents were far more common than they had been even in 1500. This helped the landowning classes to indulge in fairly obvious ostentatious spending whether on castles and stately homes of all shapes and sizes or the accoutrements to go in them. A Scottish landowner, as elsewhere, was judged by the extent and quality of his hospitality, and the expansion of wadsetting – effectively mortgaging parcels of lands as surety for a debt – was often a direct result of the discrepancy between lifestyle and income. The inflationary downside of feu-farming started to kick in and landed incomes, including the Crown's, began to fall. But we can certainly say that the Reformation didn't curtail the livelier side of elite living.

After 1600 it becomes considerably easier for historians to assess many elements of economic and social life, aspects so difficult for the medieval period. In basic economic terms, the period from 1580 to c.1640 was better than the period between 1660 and 1690. And the 1690s were just dreadful. Still, despite the tediousness of the basic Scottish diet – based on oatmeal and dairy products, supplemented by fish and, for the well-off, meat – the population could usually get enough to eat except in the worst years of shortage.

Three main issues dominated the reign of James VI: royal finances, church government and the English succession. The first was, of course, a perennial problem for the Stewarts (except, perhaps, his mother, who had her French dower and the first windfalls of the acquisition of church land and property by the Crown). The basic problem revolved round the fact that incomes, particularly from land, were falling, while the cost of royal government was increasing dramatically. There was just so much more for a monarch to do these days, not to mention the expense associated with acting and entertaining like a king. By now taxation was more or less regular in Scotland; the price was, as it had long been in England, a degree of parliamentary supervision of royal finances.

The second issue was one that James felt extremely strongly about, with his stance exhibited firmly under the banner of 'No bishops, no king'. For a monarch, particularly such a godly one as he claimed to be, the hierarchical structure of episcopacy was fundamental for, without it, the king would lose almost all control over the church. For the presbyterians the issue was just as entrenched: why should James exert such influence over the kirk of which he was merely another member? Towards the end of his reign, as a result of his experiences in England, the king tried to push on Scotland the kind of doctrinal practices that proved so controversial in the reign of his son. Accusations of popery were the predictable reaction, but what was at stake was the nation's identity and freedom to choose how to worship (so long as it was overtly Protestant) in the face of the ambiguity caused by James's departure for London in 1603.

James VI was at least as obsessed as his mother had been with Elizabeth's throne. Despite the Virgin Queen's longstanding determination not to name her successor, it was clear to most English politicians that the Protestant Scottish king was by far the best option

The young James VI (above and above right) inherited many problems, not the least of them being the rising cost of government (coin of James VI shown below). Also a source of concern was the pursuit of James's claim to the throne of England, given that Elizabeth I (right), the 'Virgin Queen', left no direct heirs.

James VI at the age of fifty-five, now the proud ruler of both Scotland and England, not to mention Wales and Ireland.

and when she finally died there was really very little debate over the issue. What was far more problematic was how this new King of a Greater Britain was going to divide his time between his kingdoms. Needless to say, and despite his promises (and, no doubt, his intention), Scotland only saw the return of king and court on one occasion between 1603 and James's death in 1625 – in 1618. Government now resided with the Scottish parliament, the Privy Council and the king's own apparently all-powerful pen in London. In reality, the extent to which the king was proactive in legislating for his native kingdom, as opposed to acquiescing in the policies put forward by his agents in Edinburgh, was soon negligible, with the exception of his unfortunate attempts to impose English styles of worship on the Scots. The portents for the future were very mixed indeed.

The Scots were naturally proud that James now ruled in London, that their king had succeeded in taking over the southern kingdom in a bloodless change of dynasty after so many centuries on the receiving end of English take-over bids. But they certainly didn't share King James's enthusiasm for turning Britain from a vague concept into a reality. The

The conspirators in the famous 'Gunpowder Plot' of 1605, in part an anti-Scottish reaction to James's accession.

English were even less keen. Throughout the seventeenth century, there was fundamental resistance to the idea of a closer union from English economic interests, frightened of a flood of cheap Scottish goods. But in the short term, the English nobility reacted to the perceived undue influence of Scots around 'their' king in much the same way as English politicians did in 1997 when Tony Blair's Labour cabinet also appeared to be full of the prime minister's countrymen. We shouldn't forget that Guy Fawke's plan to blow up the House of Lords in 1605, though first and foremost a Catholic plot, was also about sending the Scots back from whence they had come.

Edinburgh was very worried that the loss of the court would make a huge dent in both the capital's reputation and its economic well being – the semi-constant presence of king and nobility had resulted in the spending of large amounts of money. In fact, many of the mercahnts, financiers and businessmen of Edinburgh continued to accumulate great wealth. The loss to the country was ameliorated in the short-term by the fact that James was, first and foremost, the king of Scots. But the stage was set for the very real difficulty of how Scotland's interests were going to be served by future monarchs who had neither a great knowledge of, nor interest in, their northern kingdom.

In the meantime, James earnestly set about trying to bring peace and harmony to parts of his realm that were far from settled. In particular he attacked what had now become the 'Middle Shires' but which are more usually known as the borders. And he also instigated various plans to get to grips with the Highlands. The enforced removal of troublesome families was one strategy that was applied to both areas. Another venture was the attempted plantation of 'civilized' Lowlanders in the Isle of Lewis, but this was spectacularly unsuccessful. The borders began to settle down but with the Highlands the problem was compounded by both distance and a fundamental clash of culture.

James attempted to force the highlanders to abandon their 'barbaric' Irish ways through legislation (the Statutes of Iona, 1609), which was hardly the right tactic with which to effect the area's final effective integration into mainstream Scotland. It would also be true to say that much of the unrest in the area was a result of Crown policy in the past, either through direct action or the use of royal agents such as the earls of Argyll. But in the meantime, an outbreak of action on the part of government, either in Edinburgh or London, was still likely to have little or no impact over the longer term because of the lack of will to commit long-term resources to the 'problem'.

Another interesting feature of the reign of James VI was the first hints of a commercial interest in the highlands, from both within and outwith the region. The king granted a number of monopolies, primarily to his master of the mint, Nathanial Edwart (not a native of these parts), who then co-operated with key Scottish nobles like Sir George Hay, later earl of Kinnoull. They attempted, among other things, to exploit salt, iron and timber in a much more determined fashion than had been obvious previously. Though their efforts met with only limited success, so far as we can tell, perhaps their main legacy was the example that they provided for native highland nobility, such as the Mackenzie earl of Seaforth and the Campbell earl of Breadalbane, to involve their own estates in such enterprises. That was to prove a very significant development indeed.

James died in 1625 and was succeeded by his son Charles. A native of Scotland – he was born in Dunfermline – this eighth Stewart monarch had lived out his childhood in the

Kilchurn Castle, seat of the Campbell earl of Breadalbane, was the centre of increasing entrepreneurial activity from the seventeenth century.

shadow of his elder brother, Henry, and (perhaps like his great-great-great-grandfather James III) lacked the necessary charisma to manage the nobility. Part of Charles's problem (just like James III) was that he didn't feel that he needed to manage anyone – he was king and would therefore do what he thought was best, regardless.

If the Scots thought they had had problems with James VI trying to interfere in the way they should worship God, this was nothing compared with what Charles I wanted them to do. As the 1630s progressed, the gulf between the king and his godly people in matters of religion widened even further. Of course, Charles's intransigence wasn't restricted to the Scots, but their increasing tendency towards Presbyterianism made the monarch's perceived leanings towards Rome appear even more unpalatable. He was also adept at offending the very people on whom his government in Scotland fundamentally relied: the nobility.

Charles I (right) did not become heir to the dual throne until 1612, when his elder brother, Henry Prince of Wales (below), was truck down by typhoid.

Charles I in full majesty, as portrayed by Sir Anthony van Dyck.

Relations deteriorated even further after Charles actually visited his northern kingdom in 1633 – any hopes that the personal touch would help to calm things down were proved sadly mistaken. In fact, the king's behaviour during a parliament held in his presence in that year led the nobility to believe that the problems went even deeper. The heart of their concerns was the very freedom of the Scottish parliament itself: circumspect monitoring of who voted for what was one thing; Charles's open note-taking was another. The trial and conviction of Lord Balmerino for treason in 1635 for, among other things, criticizing the way things were handled in 1633 left the country seething. It only needed a spark to blow Scotland apart.

In the meantime, Charles forced through the theoretical acceptance of his beloved English prayerbook and the Scots prepared for the first church service at which the hated object would be used. From 1637 the road to war was, if not inevitable, at least being planned. The king himself must take a large share of the blame, though much of what he was trying to do had been implicit in his father's policies too. Scotland, where government until 1603 had relied so much on the personal regulatory and conciliatory presence of the monarch, was already finding out that the price of the regal union with England might be too high.

The so-called Bishops' War broke out in 1639. As with the final push towards the Reformation itself, the religious and the nationalist camps had combined in a holy alliance to save kirk and country, united under the banner of the National Covenant which so many of Scotland's nobles, intellectuals and lawyers – the upper and middle classes – had signed.

The Scots enjoyed some unaccustomed military success during this period, invading Ireland and occupying parts of northern England thanks to the generalship of men like Alexander Leslie, who had reached the dizzying heights of Field Marshal in the Swedish army before events at home called him back. But this was at least as much a civil as a national war. Most particularly, the earl of Argyll took the opportunity to continue the process of Campbellizing the highlands. His enemies were a loose confederation led by the dashing ex-Covenanter the Marquis of Montrose and including the equally romantic Alastair MacColla – Colkitto – who brought a force of Catholic Irish to join their fellow Gaels in some of the bloodiest episodes of the pre-Cromwell phase of the wars. This Celtic element endured, at best, an uneasy partnership with Lowland soldiers, but the Highland charge was crucial to the success which they initially enjoyed. However, the soldiers were fighting for different things – the somewhat contradictory rights of the Protestant religion and the Stewart monarchy in Montrose's case, and the heritage of the MacDonald lords of the Isles against the usurping Campbells for the Gaels. The confederation lasted until 1645 when Montrose was caught out at the battle of Philiphaugh.

The Covenanting Wars of the 1640s and '50s were an extraordinary period in what was, perhaps for the first time, a genuinely British history. The three kingdoms of Scotland, England and Ireland certainly all interfered directly in each other's affairs and it is hard to write the history of one without referring to the others. To begin with, Charles's enemies in Scotland and England looked as if they could make a common cause after the outbreak of civil war in England in 1642. However, the Scots' insistence on a Presbyterian-based union with England, combined with the English parliament's failure to meet its financial promises to the Scottish army, strained relationships.

Commanders of the Covenanting Wars. Left to right: Archibald Campbell, 8th earl of Argyll, for whom the wars as ever provided an opportunity to further his own ends in the highlands; Alexander Leslie, who returned from Sweden to fight with the Covenanters; James Graham, earl of Montrose, the dashing commander of Royalist forces in the highlands.

Threave Castle on the River Dee, once the stronghold of the Black Douglases, has lain in ruins since it was taken by the Covenanters in 1640 following a thirteen-week siege.

But the common purpose that had underpinned the anti-royalist cause disintegrated completely once the king had surrendered to the Scots in 1646. Many in England and Scotland wanted to work towards an accommodation with Charles, but his capture by English radicals – the New Model Army – in June 1647 put everyone at each other's throats. The Scots, however furious they were with the closed mind of Charles I, certainly never had any intention of removing it permanently from his body. Once Oliver Cromwell's puritans had executed the King of England in 1649, forgetting that he was also the King of Scots, the lines of engagement were drawn under more usual national lines.

Despite initial successes, the Covenanters had already begun to experience military reversals in the wider British wars. And each time they did so, extreme Presbyterians argued that this only indicated God's displeasure and the need for purges of the ungodly. After the defeat of those supporting accommodation with Charles at Preston in 1648, the kirk party finally found no-one left in Scotland to argue with them and their day had come.

Whether the nobility liked it or not, a Pandora's box of potential social upheaval which had been on the table since the reformation was now open, however temporarily. The country's elites had been much exercised about the threat to parliament and political autonomy, including, but not exclusively, the issue of religious freedom that acted as the catalyst for the wars in the first place. But for many people operating outside the central political sphere, the religious issue was fundamentally linked to social change. Presbyterianism had at its core a belief in equality and it didn't take a huge stretch of the imagination to transfer beliefs supposedly related to the afterlife into the here and now. Between 1648 and 1650, power lay with the godly and even the Scottish nobility faced the dreadful ignominy of being hauled up by the kirk session for their immoral activities.

But this continual cleansing and purging did little for national unity and certainly nothing for the army's performance. Charles's execution united the Scots and the tide began to turn against the radicals within Scotland, not to mention the radicals in England. The heir to the throne was immediately proclaimed as Charles II, King of Scots but the seriously purged Scottish army was no match for Cromwell's forces. Even the great General Leslie could not prevent a categorical defeat at Dunbar for the second time in Scottish history in September 1650. The finale came a year later at Worcester, when an invading Scottish army was defeated along with other Royalists and the newly crowned

Having withstood a sustained assault by Royalist forces under Montrose, Castle Campbell (or Castle Gloom as it was at the time) was occupied by Cromwell's forces following his victory at Dunbar. This was not the expected reward for the Covenanter earl of Argyll.

Charles II was forced to hide up an oak tree (allegedly). There is a curious irony in the fact that the Scots began these wars against Charles I but ended up on the losing side supporting the crown.

The Cromwellian occupation of Scotland is one of the most traumatic and uncomfortable episodes in Scottish history. The country endured ten years of occupation of a kind that Edward I could only dream about. A number of Scottish towns – Ayr, Leith, Perth, Inverness, Inverloch – still bear the mark of the New Model Army's presence in the remains of fortifications of various sizes. The Scots, who had tried in the previous decade to join with England in a Presbyterian union, now got their wish, much to their horror, and without their beloved Presbyterianism. The Scottish parliament was abolished and a 'Commonwealth of England, Scotland and Ireland' proclaimed. But this was an enforced union, and parliament – the protector of liberties and mouthpiece of the wider nation – had now become the very symbol of oppression.

Cromwellian government in Scotland also bore another close relationship to previous English administrations in the northern kingdom – its cost. The total direct tax bill topped £90,000 per year, in comparison to the £17,000 demanded by Charles I. It should also be remembered that the Scots had spent over a decade at war, at a considerable cost to its land, economy and people. Superficially, the Cromwellian experiment was extremely impressive in its thoroughness. The nobility of Scotland were still out in the cold, their very legal authority at a local level abolished. But it was too much too soon. After Protector Cromwell's death in 1658, it was only a matter of time before 'normality' was resumed.

The military strength of Oliver Cromwell (left) allowed him to treat Scotland with impunity. Fortunately, his son Richard (right), though groomed to succeed him, lacked his father's capabilities and was denied his role as Lord Protector.

Charles II as pictured by Samuel Cooper and in a coin of his reign.

Many Scots, especially those usually described as the 'middling sort', approved of the union, but wanted it fundamentally renegotiated to be a fairer, more equal partnership. With Charles II's restoration in 1660, their voice, which had been so unusually prominent in the previous decades, was severely quietened. However, it was hard to shut them up completely once they had played such a dominant role. The lairds and the burghs, dominated by merchants and the growing professional classes such as lawyers, together with the ministers, had taken over the direction of national affairs to an unprecedented extent during the period of the Covenanting wars. It was not an experience they were likely to forget.

With the restoration of the Stewarts, the old question of the church hierarchy reasserted itself almost immediately. The triumph of Presbyterianism, so much a part of what the Covenanters had fought for, had to be atoned for in the quest for normality. And so the bishops came back, along with the nobility.

A minimal amount of blood-letting also accompanied the return of the traditional regime. Archibald Johnston of Wariston, the Edinburgh lawyer partly responsible for drafting the 1639 Covenant, together with the Protestant minister James Guthrie and the redoubtable Argyll were all executed. The Restoration regime in Scotland was characterized by its desire to re-establish the political status quo as if the 1640s and '50s

The Scottish Maiden was a feature of the Scots legal system in the sixteenth and seventeenth centuries and the last visit of many of Scotland's most colourful characters. The 8th earl of Argyll, beheaded in Edinburgh in 1660, is said to have called the guilltoine 'the sweetest maiden I have ever kissed'.

had never happened. Even Charles was probably pleasantly surprised by how acquiescent the Scottish authorities seemed anxious to be.

The biggest flashpoint continued to be ostensibly religious. For the first time in Scottish history we hear directly from ordinary men and women articulating their own needs and aspirations. With the re-establishment of episcopalianism in 1662, progress, so far as they were concerned, had not just been halted but effectively binned. Led bya few hundred dissenting ministers, these Presbyterian faithful took to the fields and hills to worship in conventicles and to call into question the whole framework of the society they lived in. The movement was prevalent throughout the lowlands, but its main stronghold was the south-west.

The government was far from amused. Its driving force was insecurity and that led it to take extremely firm measures against this religious and social dissent, despite the fact that the vast majority supported the Restoration settlement agreed with Charles in 1661-2. The king, now firmly re-established in London, was faced with the fundamental problem of post-1603 politics: which of his advisers, those closest to him or those operating in Scottish circles, to follow in the absence of his own first-hand knowledge of the Scottish situation.

The earl of Lauderdale (left) was given considerable responsibility in Scotland after Charles II's restoration and did much to stabilize the political situation alongside ex-Covenanters such as (who else?) Archibald Campbell, 9th earl and 1st duke of Argyll (right).

From 1662 onwards he relied on a man who effectively became Scotland's first prime minister: John Maitland, 2nd earl of Lauderdale. Lauderdale worked, to begin with at least, in partnership with Archibald Campbell, earl of Argyll, who, as ever and despite his father's execution, acted as the Crown's agent in the highlands. As ever, too, Crown policy in the highlands looked remarkably like Campbell self-interest.

The government's severity towards the conventicling movement was a response partly to the implied social agenda of their protagonists, and also to a security fear in England thanks to the outbreak of a number of European conflicts, including the Anglo-Dutch wars. So far as the English were concerned, since Scotland was still independent it posed a significant security threat as a potential ally of the southern kingdom's many enemies abroad. The Scottish government did try toleration on a number of occasions but its reaction to outbreaks of revolt in 1666 and 1679 was heavy-handed to put it mildly. However, by the time of the last revolt of the reign these radical Presbyterians were, like the government itself, deeply divided about what to do next, and the heyday of the early 1670s when 10,000 conventiclers enjoyed open-air worship in the south-west was already over.

But the Restoration government was not wholly insensitive to some aspects of interregnum politics. Lauderdale, for example, with the support of Scotland's economic interests, including the burghs, tried to broker a commercial union with England. However, the English, with their expanding colonial empire to protect, wanted none of it.

Dunnottar Castle (above), in whose dungeons (right) insurgent Covenanters were imprisoned and killed during the unrest of the late seventeenth century.

What this boiled down to was the fact that many of the fundamental problems related to having two kingdoms and one king were at least as problematic in the second half of the seventeenth century as they had been earlier on. The increasingly complex European military situation was one contributing factor. However, the commercial opportunities opening up across the Atlantic, from which the Scots were excluded, was perhaps an even greater source of resentment. It is seriously to be doubted whether a pre-1603 Scotland could have done any better without a large navy, but the problem was perhaps that the

Scots could see very clearly, because of their close asociation with England, exactly what they were missing.

The whole tenor of Restoration politics was emphatically based on a desire not to rock the boat. However, the viability of such a policy was severely tested with the accession to the throne of King James VII of Scotland (II of England) in 1685. Where Charles may have had certain sympathies towards Catholicism, his brother wore them defiantly on his sleeve, together with the worst type of Stewart autocratic tendencies. Most of the Scottish nobility felt excluded from the king's inner circle; indeed, some, like Argyll, went so far as to live abroad, maintaining something approaching a Scottish political and cultural elite in exile in the Protestant Netherlands particularly. At home, however, the nobility as a whole was still extremely reticent about taking the fundamental steps needed to actually change the situation. And so, yet again, the fate of the monarch, not to mention Scotland itself, rested on events in England.

James VII took Stewart arrogance to an extreme, reulting in the alienation of nobles like the all-important earl of Argyll.

William II of Scotland and III of England (left), whose marriagee to Mary Stewart (right), James's daughter, gave him the opportunity to make a claim for his father-in-law's throne.

The English tolerated yet another Stewart intransigent for three years before encouraging the arrival of James's son-in-law, William of Orange (a province in the Protestant Netherlands), seeking the throne. A month or so later, on 23 December 1688 the king fled the country. Scotland largely held its breath, though there was sufficient anti-Catholic feeling to prompt a riot in Edinburgh which specifically targeted James's newly kitted-out chapel in Holyrood Abbey. However, the king's own bullying attempts to persuade the Scottish parliament to maintain the male Stewart line in its homeland failed in contrast to William's diplomatic and measured wooing.

The price of support for William II of Scotland was the re-establishment of Presbyterianism as the national religion, though that form of Protestantism was by no means welcome in all parts of the country. However, William cared little for Scotland itself after the initial negotiations for his acquisition of its crown.

In some ways this facet of seventeenth-century political life helped to make the nation more self-reliant and even entrepreneurial. Up to a point, the Scots were free to develop mechanisms and institutions to promote and enhance economic activity, despite the ultimate handicap of a lack of royal leadership and support. The establishment of the Bank of Scotland in 1695, only a year after the Bank of England and by the same Scot, William

Paterson, is an example of the kind of initiative for which the nation would soon be world renowned.

Scotland at the end of the seventeenth century was riddled with contradictions. Economically, the commitment to economic innovation and enterprise was high in some quarters, yet the country itself faced near ruin, thanks to a series of appalling harvests and the sinking of much of the nation's capital in the ruinous Darien scheme. This attempt to finally develop a colony of Scotland's own on the isthmus of Panama was, at best, hampered by the fact that the territory in question was already claimed by Spain. The king had agreed to the endeavour in part because of the outcry against the government thanks to the Massacre of Glencoe (see below). However, the withdrawal of both English and Dutch financial support left the venture severely lacking in capital even before it started. The terrible climate and unfriendliness of the neighbouring Spanish then combined to finish it off. This blow to Scottish finances and confidence was to have long-term repercussions.

Internally, the country was perhaps no less disunited than it had ever been. However, a significant change had taken place in one important aspect during the century. The Covenanting wars had forged the destiny of the highlands perhaps at least as much as the subsequent adherence (far from uniform) to the house of Stewart. From the 1640s the area had finally taken part en masse in national politics, however much local politics had also been involved. And with this growing connection to national affairs, the economic trends which affected the rest of Britain would also have an impact on the highlands. The same rules did not necessarily apply to both the Highlands and the Lowlands, but at least they were now both playing the same game. The outcry surrounding the Massacre of Glencoe is indicative of this very fact: it is impossible to imagine a similar result of government policy having such a negative effect in the south of the country in previous centuries.

The Massacre of 1692 was a product both of the kind of policies long implemented in the area by kings determined to bring forms of justice usual in the Lowlands to bear in the Highlands and of government insecurity at the area's overall preference for the Stewart line. The MacDonalds of Glencoe were by no means the worst offenders as Jacobites but they were an easy target and were generally regarded as the kind of cattle thieves that, presumably, no one would really miss. The billeting of government soldiers on the village of Glencoe prior to the killings is, understandably, generally regarded as the worst aspect of the whole botched affair, a betrayal of highland hospitably in a most cruel and cynical way. Blame has been easily apportioned but the policy itself was no better or worse than many other government attempts to control the Highlands, which usually attempted – and usually failed – to change the Highland way of doing things. In the longer term, the outcry did not change that overall policy, though it did, as already mentioned, help in the formation of the ,Company of Scotland, which got involved in Darien.

Scotland does seem to have changed quite a bit between 1560 and 1700, though, to be fair, so had the world. Religion had now entered ordinary men and women's lives as an active social and political activity. This did not just affect politics and social relations. However, it's difficult to point to what might be termed a national culture. The culture of the Covenanters and the conventiclers was local and non-elite, not just because these movements encompassed the lower orders of society in a proactive role for the first time. More important was the fact that Edinburgh in particular no longer operated as the home of the royal court, the number one source of patronage and encouragement for national arts and culture. Of course, local culture should be just as Scottish as elite culture but it hasn't tended to be viewed that way for this non-democratic society.

It was difficult for Scotland to adjust to its new status within the Union of the Crowns. Independent, but inevitably affected by the more demanding needs of its larger neighbour, the nation tried hard to modernize, particularly in terms of some aspects of economic development. But it was difficult to overcome considerable barriers, both home grown and intrinsic to the new situation. It was not obvious where Scotland's best interests lay – to continue to press for an economic union with England or to go it completely alone. But the need for a resolution of some kind was becoming more and more pressing.

NINE

Scotland in Britain

1702 – 1850

The political union between Scotland and England was one of the biggest talking points for twentieth-century Scots. Even in 1998, when Scotland voted to re-establish a parliament in Edinburgh, the situation did not revert back to the position it had been before the union of 1707. It couldn't: Scotland, and the United Kingdom, is now a democracy and the sovereign wields only symbolic power. But in the early eighteenth century questions relating to the monarchy were fundamental to the whole relationship between Scotland and England – and nearly blew the union of the Crowns apart.

The question of who should rule Scotland was problematic even before the death of King William. The exiled James VII had been welcomed in Catholic France, eager to cause aggravation to its deadly enemy, England. The first Jacobite campaign within Scotland had taken place as early as 1689, when John Graham of Claverhouse ('Bonnie' Dundee) used the Highland charge to great effect at Killiecrankie before he was killed by a stray bullet. The reasons behind support for Jacobitism are complex and will be dealt with below. Suffice to say that internal security was something that disturbed both the Scottish and the English governments.

John Graham, Viscount Dundee, who continued to fight for James's cause until his death at the battle of Killiecrankie in 1689.

When William died in 1702, he was succeeded by his sister-in-law, Anne, the second and surviving daughter of James VII (William had been married to the elder daughter, Mary). That posed little difficulty for the Scots – she was a genuine Stewart after all – but there were bound to be problems ahead since poor Anne's many children all predeceased her.

England still hadn't learned any lessons from previous flashpoints between the two countries, most obviously the execution of Charles I. Some acknowledgement of the fact that the English monarch also ruled an independent Scotland would not have gone amiss. However, the English went right ahead and chose as heir to the English throne a descendant of James VI's daughter, Elizabeth of Bohemia, George, the elector of Hanover. The Scots actively contemplated choosing someone else, passing an act in parliament allowing them to do just that and thereby break the union of the Crowns, but in reality they had little choice, since George was the nearest Protestant member of the Stewart family. Most people in Scotland did not really want the Catholic Stewarts back, but it would have been nice to be asked.

The succession was not the only source of difficulty between the two kingdoms. Access to imperial markets was another issue of critical importance and the losses sustained at Darien only made it even more essential to find a solution to England's determination to keep the Scots out. Equally importantly, Scotland was determined not to get involved in yet another costly and, so far as the northern kingdom was concerned, pointless European war engaged upon by England. However, in reality, they were severely limited by the lack of support from a monarch whose first priority was always the greater glory that came with England's interests. Scotland seems to have known what it wanted but did not have the power and influence to get it.

The union is a very difficult subject to discuss because, as with all political situations, it excites extremes of opinion, most of which are perfectly valid. As ever, though, an incorporating union with England was not inevitable until late on in proceedings. Having said that, Scotland was becoming increasingly fed up with the constitutional situation resulting from James VI's accession to the English throne in 1603 and, to be honest, something needed to be done. Union was only one option, however, and in the years immediately following 1700 it looked far more likely that the Scots would try to go it alone once more.

James VI would have been proud of his great-granddaughter, Anne, for she, like him, wanted a proper political union between the two countries. However, Anne was not remotely interested in this constitutional change from Scotland's point of view – she was determined to have it to secure the southern kingdom from the threat posed by Scotland

Queen Anne with her son William, duke of Gloucester. Like her other children, William predeceased his mother, leaving George of Hanover as the heir to the British throne.

as a potential ally of England's enemies. In this respect, nothing much had changed since the time of Edward I. Negotiations began in 1705, encouraged by a comparatively new force in English politics, the constitutionally forward-looking Whig party. Its rival, the Tory party, was still deeply suspicious of the impact on England of a union with their far less commercially successful neighbour.

In Scotland, there is no doubt that the whole project was deeply unpopular throughout the kingdom as a whole, even with those, like the merchants, who might have been expected to welcome the new opportunities that union promised. But, as already mentioned, this was no democracy and it shouldn't be judged as if it was. Another key issue, which still causes huge arguments, was the role played by the Scottish nobility. Were they, as Robert Burns so eloquently argued in one of his songs, 'bought and sold for English gold'?. Money certainly changed hands but much of it was legitimately owed – to those who had not been paid their full salaries for occupying government posts, for example.

Many, both then and now, could argue that union undoubtedly served Scotland's best interests, in the economic sphere at least. Others point to the political cost to Scotland, the union's basic unpopularity and the damage done to the nation's self-esteem, though this was not necessarily immediately apparent. However, the fact of the matter is that on 16 January 1707 the Scottish parliament voted itself out of existence and the reluctant Scottish bride finally succumbed to her equally ambivalent southern suitor, for better or worse.

The problem for those who supported union, for whatever reason, was the fact that for a considerable period after 1707 the advantages to Scotland were not at all obvious. Despite an agreement to pay £398,085 10s sterling as compensation for, among other things, the terrible losses sustained by many Scots in the Darien fiasco, many received nothing for years. Difficulties with the economy were not particular to Scotland, though the country had suffered terribly in the famine years of the 1690s and this was exacerbated by increasing protectionism in England and, of course, the loss of capital and confidence in Darien. It was not until the middle of the eighteenth century that the Scots finally felt the benefit of joining forces with England through the profits to be made from markets increasingly available in the growing colonial empire.

In the meantime, many in this embryonic British state soon felt that the 1707 political solution to the particular problems of the first years of the eighteenth century had been a mistake. Within six years a motion had been presented to the House of Lords in Westminster to dissolve the union where it failed by only one vote (though admittedly the bill was unlikely to get through the Commons).

In Scotland, the threat of French intervention on behalf of the exiled Stewarts had by no means diminished. The first uprising struck while the iron was hot, in 1708, when a small French fleet carried the Pretender himself – James VIII, son of James VII – to Scotland. Despite the notoriety attached to the last Jacobite rising of 1745-6, this one carried the best chance of success because of the sentiment that it could tap into. Bad luck and some bad judgement meant that the fleet never landed but it was generally believed

James Stuart, the Pretender, (above and right, as a child with his sister Louisa) was the cause of uprisings in 1708 and later when his adherents, the Jacobites, attempted to restore him to the Scottish throne.

that it would have attracted widespread support if it had. The government of Anne – the last Stewart monarch – was becoming very nervous indeed.

The Westminster government, with its overtly English concerns, helped to store up trouble in the north. This was by no means intended but it proved difficult to avoid. Within a year of the union, the Scottish privy council, the main mechanism of executive power since the king left in 1603, was abolished. Government had well and truly moved out of Scotland and it remained to be seen what would take its place in managing the northern kingdom effectively.

But in other ways Scotland maintained some of its independence, despite these huge changes in government and administration. Its legal and education system, not to mention its church, remained separate and these institutions would provide much of the focus for a definite, not to mention defiant, Scottish identity. Westminster legislation might not have been welcome in its effects on many aspects of Scottish society, though the burghs generally welcomed a more British economic policy. There was enough latitude to ensure a growing commitment to a developing Britain as the economic picture eventually began to change for the better for many Scots. But not yet.

Queen Anne died in 1714. It was the end of an era. The Stewart dynasty had produced twelve monarchs and survived for over 300 years. In romance and mythology, not to mention the odd rebellion, it would survive for a bit longer yet. Anne's Hanoverian

George I, elector of Hanover before acceding to the British throne in 1715.

cousin eventually arrived in London in 1715 to become the first George in British history. The fact that he did not even speak English augured badly for Scotland, which was rarely much of a priority in London at the best of times. The change of regime meant a clean sweep in royal advisers and one of those who lost out, the earl of Mar, took the opportunity to stir up continuing dissatisfaction in a second Jacobite rising. James Stewart across the water had lost out to a German in 1715 – there was little chance of a Stewart return to the throne of England so long as the exiled dynasty remained Catholic. But some maintained a nostalgia for 'their' royal family, especially if they were episcopalian or Catholic.

Despite overwhelming numbers, Mar managed to botch the military encounters with government troops. The Pretender was despatched on yet another boat for Scotland and even managed to touch land this time. But it was too late to turn Mar's indifferent campaigning into a solid base of support. This would be the last rising that represented something approximating a Scottish reaction to the political status quo. The highlands had always played a prominent role in Jacobite uprisings but after 1715 the cause could be defined by its support from the north-west. The time for attracting lowland sympathies through the unpopularity of the union was running out.

The highlands were now in a difficult position. Before the Covenanting wars, the area had tended to impinge only indirectly on the wider Scottish, or British, political order. Disorder in the north-west particularly was regarded as a nuisance by the government, but the latter's own activities tended to be the catalyst to overt bad behaviour (as those in the south saw it). The highlands were largely left alone. That all changed in the mid-seventeenth century when the highlanders joined in the British wars of that period and became a part of British politics at the same time. Not all clans were Jacobite by any manner of means. But they were all effectively on one side (King James) or the other (King George) on this issue, which was more than just a highland or even a Scottish one. The fact that the highlanders were reacting to long-standing grievances, the most important of which was the free rein given to the duke of Argyll to dominate all aspects of life in the highlands, is not really the point. The clock could not be turned back.

The idea that the highlands were stuck in some kind of archaic Golden Age of an older, simpler and somehow purer way of life would be quite wrong. On the other hand, there's no doubt that this was a distinct culture and society whose primary resource was the manpower that had traditionally supplied warriors. But in the seventeenth century the economic potential of the highlands was finally noted by both native chiefs and southern entrepreneurs. As already mentioned, the latter proved unable, as yet, to make much of the available opportunities. Even the York Buildings Company, set up in the aftermath of the 1715 with estates forfeited from Jacobite sympathizers, couldn't make a go of it. But many native highland landowners were both willing and able to exploit the natural resources – predominantly cattle, timber and fish – of their estates.

There is no denying Campbell resourcefulness. On the very eve of the final Jacobite rebellion in 1745 one Campbell enterprise – the Loch Etive trading company – was busy

The fortunes of the Campbell clan continued to prosper in the early eighteenth century. John Campbell, 2nd duke of Argyll, (left) continued his family's dominance in the highlands, doing well from the demise of those who, like George Keith, Earl Marischal, (right) were attainted for their part in the 1715 rebellion.

dealing in tobacco and other luxury goods up and down the west coast. Another Campbell, the earl of Breadalbane, among many others, had sold most of his stock of timber on his western estates to a group of Irish entrepreneurs in the 1720s and '30s.

But other clan chiefs found themselves out in the cold. Cameron of Lochiel, for example, discovered that he was unable to break into these new markets as fully as he wished because he did not have the backing of the Campbells or any other important Scottish magnates. This may partly explain why he was tempted into supporting the Pretender one last time in 1745.

But conditions in the highlands can't be blamed on centuries of Campbell dominance alone – that only affected certain parts for a start. The lack of infrastructure, distance from markets and extreme poverty of an area which did not lack natural resources but which had sustained itself for so long on the military potential of its people made it very difficult to adjust to the new world of colonialism and commercialization. Economic considerations are not the whole story, but highland support for the Jacobite cause was by no means based entirely on nostalgia. Many had already been trying to adjust in the seventeenth century, but the pace of change seemed to be speeding up in the eighteenth. And that caused inevitable friction.

Despite an increasing diffidence towards Jacobitism, support for the union in the lowlands was still far from assured even into the 1720s. The issue that caused the biggest outrage in that decade was one that hit the Scotsman where it hurt most – his pocket and his liquor. Despite assurances in the union treaty that Scotland would not suffer from an excess of taxation, a Malt Tax (which affected the sale of beer) was introduced in 1725, resulting in serious rioting in the burghs. The government initially found it difficult to distinguish between economic uncertainty provoking unrest in the lowlands and more deep-seated problems in the highlands, so one of the main planks of its policy in Scotland was the appointment of General Wade who took on the job of mapping the highlands and beginning the building of an infrastructure of roads and garrisons to finally integrate the north-west with the rest of the country. Finally, however, the government realized that something needed to be done to stimulate the Scottish economy as a whole and in 1727 a Board of Trustees was set up to promote fishing and manufacturing industries.

The Scottish nobility, particularly those who found themselves politically redundant because of the decrease in the numbers who could attend the London – as opposed to the Edinburgh – parliament, took some time to adjust to their new role. For those who were able to take part in Westminster politics, being a British politician meant spending long periods in the south, inevitably involving another leap in expenditure commensurate with maintaining a house in the capital, not to mention the lifestyle to go with it. This had a particular impact on the highlands where, eventually, absentee landlords began to develop fundamentally different priorities to traditional ones, thanks to the things they learned in London and their own decreasing knowledge of the day-to-day management of their estates. Changes in attitude did not happen overnight, nor were they by any means uniform, but it all helped eventually to bring about a fundamental transformation.

Scotland itself had to cope with a new form of political management, as the Westminster government adjusted to accommodating the needs of the northern kingdom without compromising on England's requirements. As already indicated, there was considerable paranoia about security threats fuelled by the confusion of Jacobitism, the European wars and anti-union sentiment in the first decades after 1707. But slowly the government got better at handling the situation, though this didn't preclude continuing paranoia. Archibald Campbell, earl of Islay (later Duke of Argyll), emerged as the first post-union political manager of note in the 1720s, maintaining his position off and on for the next forty years. Islay worked very hard for Scotland, helping to promote improvement in general and the linen industry in particular, for example. Nevertheless, instability continued to be a major element in Scottish politics.

Government attempts to control the highlands were also, as ever, about damage limitation rather than a positive response to the needs of the area. And so, yet again, a few in the highlands were tempted into supporting a man who, in reality, had little or no real commitment to protecting the distinctive, but increasingly anachronistic, lifestyle of the area. A window of opportunity opened up in 1744 when Louis XV of France decided to activate the potential of Jacobitism against England. However, by 1745 French support had dwindled to little more than the handful who landed with the Pretender's son, Prince Charles Edward Stuart, in August 1745. The temptation to send him back from whence he had come was, unfortunately, resisted.

It is difficult, with the benefit of hindsight, to understand exactly what Bonnie Prince Charlie's loyal highland supporters really thought they could achieve. It seems unlikely, even if the prince could have been persuaded to limit Stewart ambitions to Scotland, that the lowlands would have been permanently persuaded of the benefits of a Stewart restoration imposed from the north. It is significant that the rapidly developing colonial entrepreneurs of Glasgow wanted as little as possible to do with this disruptive war, though

'Bonnie Prince Charlie' as a young man (top) and as an aging and unsuccessful pretender.

many in Edinburgh became blinded by the brief nostalgic return to the glory days when a king and court lived – and spent – in style in the capital.

The conflict of interests inherent in the Jacobite army eventually led to its final dénouement at the battle of Culloden in April 1746. A fundamental split appeared the minute the army decided to cross the border into England in November 1745. The prince was determined to press on to London, but his army insisted on a return to the north just over a month later, nervous at the distance from home and the lack of expected Jacobite support in the south. Rumours of a supporting French invasion allegedly caused complete panic in London, but the Scots were perhaps right, given their long history of waiting for concrete action on the part of the French, to presume that it would never actually happen.

Even after the duke of Cumberland – George I's son – had finally put an end to the perceived invincibility of the highland charge at Culloden, many Jacobite leaders were quite prepared to rally and carry on. They organized a meeting at Ruthven barracks in the shadow of the Cairngorms – ironically one of General Wade's creations – but their prince was already making his romantic escape from the country.

Prompted perhaps by the terror that this ragtag highland army had inspired in southern England, not to mention the personal inclination of Cumberland himself, the aftermath of the '45 was supposed to be more punitive than after earlier revolts, though from the 1750s attempts were also made to stimulate the highland economy. The highlands now

Simon Fraser , Baron Lovat, chief of the Fraser clan, (left, in a painting by Hogarth) had been secretly working for the exiled Stewarts for years before being beheaded on Tower Hill for his part in the '45 rebellion. The rebels were dealt with firmly by the duke of Cumberland (above).

found itself on the receiving end of a systematic campaign to extirpate the contemporary Gaelic way of life and turn the Gael into a model citizen of the new Britain. However, the duke of Argyll, so often regarded as the villain of the piece, succeeded in blunting the edge of this racist policy, aided by the fact that most highlanders were not actually Jacobites.

From the government's point of view, the policy ultimately succeeded. The martial traditions of the highlander was channelled away from rebellion into loyal service in British imperial armies, leading to the ultimate rehabilitation of the highlands in recent times, reinvented as a romantic symbol of Scotland itself. But the cost was immense, and not just in the immediate loss of life after Culloden. So far as the vast majority of clan members were concerned, their chiefs – the natural bastion of support against central government – had profoundly let them down. But the landowners faced pressures of their own as they struggled with debt and the need to make their estates financially viable under new economic conditions. Many continued to try to accommodate the needs of their people with the growing demands of the market but as the population began to grow steeply after 1750 the contradictions became largely irreconcilable.

Leaving aside the disruption caused by the last Jacobite rebellion, the 1740s also showed signs that the Scots might finally come to enjoy better times. We should not forget that, well into the nineteenth century, Scotland's population remained overwhelmingly rural. We should also remember that the growing pace of change associated with the burgeoning industrial revolution was accompanied, if not preceded, by a transformation in rural life and work.

Despite the ostensible wealth of many members of Scottish society (not forgetting their tendency towards indebtedness as well), the vast majority of the population lived within a basic subsistence economy, as they had done for thousands of years. They produced just about enough for their communities to live on, with very little surplus (or, in bad years, a shortfall). There was little incentive or opportunity for investment, reflected in the basic, labour-intensive farming methods. Most people could barely afford to buy what they needed, never mind indulge in luxuries. It is tempting to imagine that the inhabitants of Skara Brae lived at least as well as many of their descendants nearly 5000 years later.

As members of a British aristocracy with ever-closer contacts in England, many Scottish landowners became increasingly convinced not only of the economic necessity to do things differently, but the moral one as well. Improvement, as the process of agricultural revolution is called, encompassed all the meanings of the word – landowners should engage in it as a patriotic duty to revitalize Scotland's economy, and therefore its whole future, though, as ever, practice often differed from theory. This required long-term investment, as profits were far from obvious in the first few decades of the revolution.

At the back of Improvement was a basic sort of tidymindedness, perhaps not dissimilar to the inspiration behind the church reforms accompanying the

Reformation. The current situation was a mess – from the runrig system of communal strip farming to the legal structure that supported a huge variety of tenures and accompanying rights. What the Improvers wanted, in theory, was a nice series of individual stone farms of neat fields with unambiguous property rights. In practice, however, even twenty-first-century rural landuse patterns may reflect far more ancient land divisions that were given the veneer of Improvement with fences and a degree of amalgamation.

Improvement was not purely a lowland phenomenon, though it looked rather different in the highlands. Crofting was the new, and despised, tenurial arrangement, which, as elsewhere, broke up the old townships into single-tenant blocs. Because highland leases were usually so short (one year) and other rights, including the pasturing of animals, tended to be so ancient and well-established that they were not actually written down, it was comparatively easy for landowners to sweep away the existing system. This was not yet the age of mass emigration, but the better-off could already see where the wind was blowing and left for North American pastures new of their own accord.

In the lowlands, the Improvers also did not know what to do with the whole swathe of rural workers who could not make the leap into the new world of farming. The cottars – basically farm labourers with a smallholding sufficient for the family's essential needs – were seen as a superfluous, not to mention disruptive, element. Unfortunately, there were rather a lot of them.

And it wasn't just the lowest orders of rural life that were affected by the move away from communal farming. As with feu-farming 250 years earlier, many farmers lost out because they could not afford to buy into the system and those who did manage to make the transition often found it difficult to make ends meet in increasingly competitive economic conditions. Their plight has been immortalized in the poetry of Robert Burns, who, as a tenant farmer himself, was far from convinced that such change was for the better. He had seen far too many forced off the land and others struggling to survive, while the nobility sat impervious in their big houses.

In terms of sheer numbers, the lowlands of Scotland eventually lost more people from the countryside into the growing urban environment than the highlands. It began to happen earlier, took much longer and was therefore less dramatic.

In the transition phase most still remained on the land, working in the small but numerous cottage industries that supported the expansion into linen, and later cotton, manufacture. The key point about that phase was, however, the fact that the link with agricultural employment was broken. Planned villages, like Inveraray, were not just created to provide the landowner with a pleasant view from his castle unobstructed by the sight of an untidy village below. Many were built explicitly to house those who would work in the new textile industries that began to take off in the late eighteenth century, usually operating hand-in-hand with a large town that both finished off the process and acted as a sales outlet. Then, as now, town and countryside needed to work together, however much their cultures were separate. We shouldn't be too nostalgic about the disappearance of the older villages – their inhabitants surely weren't, since

Highland cottages, Aberfoyle. From the nostalgic viewpoint of a later age, these thatched dwellings look idyllic, but life in the Highlands grew increasingly difficult as landowners changed tenurial rights and small farmers were eased out.

'The Queels' – a small croft in the parish of Huntly – was typical of the farmhouses which, by the time this photograph was taken in the late 1890s, were already on their way out, but whose introduction had caused so much grief in the previous century.

the new structures were a vast improvement on the wattle and daub structures they'd left behind.

Improvement, which included the transformation of the whole ethos behind the organization of the countryside, cannot really be divorced from the wider intellectual framework of the period. The Scottish Enlightenment allowed the nation to contribute to many areas of intellectual endeavour at a world level. However, these were no mere academic exercises: many of the new theories were found to have very practical applications that were put to good use as Scotland began to industrialize. Despite the difficulties undoubtedly experienced by the vast majority of the population, both rural and urban, the overwhelming mood of the nation at the turn of the new century was one of confidence and optimism.

David Hume is one of the best known Scottish Enlightenment figures, though also one of the most difficult to work out. Celebrated in more modern times for his alleged atheism, his philosophy was actually based on a profound desire to explain things as they really are, limiting discussions of truth to what can be proved by first-hand experience. Nevertheless, while he found favour in his own time, his views were perhaps just too advanced for the Edinburgh literati to get to grips with and though they pretended to understand them, his influence was rather limited. But his reputation after his death in 1777, when his ideas slowly began to make sense, was far greater.

The celebrated economist Adam Smith, whose work The Wealth of Nations *was an important argument for economic liberalis, was one of Scotland's many Enlightenment thinkers.*

Adam Smith is another great name to come out of the Scottish enlightenment. Best known at the end of the twentieth century for his association with the free market economics that found such favour in Britain and the US in the 1980s particularly, his magnum opus, *The Wealth of Nations*, is far more than just a handbook for rampant capitalism. Smith, like many of the Enlightenment thinkers, was profoundly influenced by the changes in society going on around him. In particular he reacted to what he saw of the activities of the tobacco lords from his position as professor of Moral Philosophy at Glasgow University, lamenting the control that these entrepreneurs exerted over most aspects of life in the city. The free market that Smith envisaged was freedom from the implacable grip of vested interests.

But Scotland's contribution was by no means restricted to the humanities. Many great discoveries were made in the sciences too. An amateur geologist, James Hutton, in the course of his detailed examinations of the rocks of the Lothian coast, was among the first to attempt a scientific, as opposed to biblical, calculation of the age of the world. Since its birth had previously been placed at 4004 BC, this must have been a great shock.

The chemist Joseph Black, who, like Smith, held a chair at Glasgow University, discovered that what had previously been regarded as fundamental chemical building blocks, such as air, were actually made up of even more basic elements. Other chemists then worked to discover them all, with useful results not just for chemistry but for the expanding new enterprises of the industrial revolution. The linen industry, for example, which took off in the mid-eighteenth century, benefited when chlorine was added to this list of primary elements. Its use as a bleaching agent allowed linen production to increase dramatically.

And, last but not least, a Scot also pioneered one of the key elements of the later industrial revolution. James Watt had worked for Joseph Black as a lab technician and some of the latter's inquisitive and pioneering spirit must have rubbed off because by 1769 Watt had made a crucial improvement to the steam engine, providing it with a separate condenser and thus vastly improving its efficiency. Once it was discovered how to make it rotate as well, the steam engine was ready for widespread use in factories and foundries throughout Scotland.

The Scottish Enlightenment is an international success story that Scots are justly proud of, coming, as it did, at a time of rising standards of living for many thanks to the early industrial revolution. And it did not just affect the intellectual elite – the emphasis on education lay close to the hearts of the growing middle classes and even the sons (usually!) of poor families occasionally had a chance to better themselves if they proved themselves academically gifted. Genteel educational establishments flourished in the growing urban centres, providing not just decent instruction for their students but also a respectable profession for schoolmasters and schoolmistresses. The Enlightenment was not just a movement, but a way of life.

By 1750 many Scots were coming round to the view that the union with England – and thus access to a growing number of markets around the world – was directly responsible for inspiring a new optimism about Scotland's economic potential. And the new economic conditions that went with these changes were also responsible for the development of a new economic powerhouse within Scotland, centred, this time, on Glasgow and the west.

In the middle ages, Glasgow had been an ecclesiastical centre focused on its cathedral and bishop (archbishop after 1492), its university and a degree of regional trade. International trade with Europe was based predominantly, and naturally, in the east coast burghs with direct access to continental markets. The Clyde, the river on which Glasgow sat, was navigable only as far as Dumbarton. So, all in all, conditions were far from favourable to major economic development.

But that reckoned without the changing dynamics of international trade, thanks to the growing importance of Britain's colonies across the Atlantic to the west, and the entrepreneurialism of Glasgow's merchants. The key to their initial success lay in their ability to exploit the expanding European market for tobacco from the Americas. By 1770, Scotland accounted for over half of the total British trade in the weed, with the so-called Glasgow tobacco lords taking the lion's share. It's no wonder they hadn't been very impressed with Bonnie Prince Charlie's antics. The road to prosperity was by no means straightforward – further outbreaks of war, including the revolt of the colonies, otherwise known as the American Wars of Independence, in the 1770s, looked as though they might jeopardize this new-found success. But in reality the growth of an independent America stabilized the situation and Scotland was soon re-established in transatlantic trade. Indeed, some historians date the real take-off in the Scottish economy as late as the 1780s.

The linen industry was the first major national success story of industrial development. It was, not, however, a factory-based enterprise, but remained in the home where the whole family could get involved, though they had distinct roles to play – only the men were actually allowed to weave the cloth on the looms. This form of industrialization was part of the transition between the traditional, land-based economy and the large-scale urban industrialization of the nineteenth century. It kept many of the population on the land who might otherwise have been forced in even larger numbers into the cities. But, as already mentioned, it broke the essential bond between the land and large numbers of the working population for the first time in Scottish history, in this case because the flax itself was mostly imported from abroad.

By the 1770s Scotland was producing over 10 million yards of cloth. Linen has less of a high profile than the cattle that still provided the backbone of the highland economy or the tobacco that catapulted Glasgow into the financial limelight. But it contributed far more to Scotland's economy as a whole and changed the lives of large numbers of Scots, nearly 10% of whom worked in the industry. One important change was the fact that the introduction of spinning made particular use of women, increasing their earning power. The pre-eminence of the linen industry was short-lived, however; only twenty years later, cotton began to take over.

Scotland's growing prosperity was based in part on its position in a triangle of imperial activity, much of which was highly immoral. Boats from the Old World sailed to Africa to pick up slaves and transported them to America and the West Indies, where they worked on the plantations that produced raw materials such as cotton, which was then transported to Britain to be processed and then exported as cloth. Though most Scottish entrepreneurs did not deal directly in slaves, they certainly reaped huge profits on the back of the dreadful business since cotton would not have been nearly so lucrative without it.

Like linen, the cotton industry did well in Scotland because wages and other costs were still comparatively low. It also helped that the population was starting to rise significantly above the one million mark around which it had fluctuated for most of the previous millennia. Even as late as the 1830s many spinners and weavers still worked at home, controlling their own lives in small rural communities. But change was creeping

These images of tweed manufacture in the 1920s and '30s echo the cottage-based production of linen and cotton in the eighteenth and nineteenth centuries, before increasing mechanization saw production shifted into the new factories.

A modern master of an older art, this man works a reconstructed loom.

Such self-employment began to disappear as workers moved into the new factories such as the famous mills at New Lanark.

on them, however slowly, paving the way towards large-scale, mechanized factories where social distinctions were transformed into the simpler, but much starker, contrast between employer and employee.

It is amazing to consider that, in the year 2000, what was until recently our basic pattern of work – the factory – has only been around for some 150 years at most. The old system was certainly riven with insecurity and the very real threat of starvation in bad years. But a man could also control his own destiny, his working hours and time off. Giving such independence away was surely a hard choice to make and it was perhaps only the lack of choice that made it remotely acceptable. Indeed, those who initially ended up in the new factories were more often women and children. Cheaper and less likely to protest about these strange new conditions – which sometimes included a prohibition on even looking out of the window – they were much more attractive than their more contumacious menfolk.

Scotland's new status as a major industrial centre is also borne out by the influx of labourers from elsewhere, including Ireland. Most settled in Glasgow and other parts of the west of Scotland, where by 1831 they made up $17\frac{1}{2}$% of the population. However, skilled Irishwomen were also attracted to the developing linen and jute industry in Dundee, where, by virtue of their fewer numbers and possibly by virtue of their sex (less threatening to men), they met with a little less hostility from the native population than in the west.

These new commercial enterprises were not the whole story, even if they did hasten the more dramatic changes in society and the economy. Nor should we imagine that industrial exploitation in Scotland began only in the eighteenth century. Many much older industries were still very important, though they also condemned their workers to horrendous conditions. Mining, for example, had been a part of the Scottish economy since at least the middle ages. In the later sixteenth century Sir George Bruce made his fortune through coal and provided James VI with one of the more novel experiences of his eventful life when he persuaded the king to walk out under the Forth through his new underground coal mine at Culross.

The treatment of those who mined the black gold is profoundly shocking. As serfs almost until the dawn of the nineteenth century in eastern Scotland, they could not leave one master for another, nor, in effect, could they choose another occupation. Even once this terrible restriction had been lifted (for economic, not moral reasons – mineowners needed more and more men to increase production), conditions did not improve, though the free miners were very well paid.

But perhaps one of the most disturbing elements of the industry was the use made of women and children. In 1842 a commission was finally set up to look into the conditions down the pits. Its report makes disturbing reading, some 150 years on. While society as a whole supposedly raised respectability into a key virtue, young girls were allowed to go down the pit to spend the long days bent double, with their skirts hiked up around their waists in the company of cursing near-naked men. The price of elegance and order was not paid by those who enjoyed it.

The eighteenth and early nineteenth centuries were not yet the high tide mark of industrialization, but major change was certainly underway. The lowlands were beginning to be dotted with factories, of which New Lanark is merely the best known. The transition from linen to cotton was not too large a step for the skilled worker, nor did it provoke major changes in working conditions. But the new iron and engineering industries that began to take off from the 1820s were a completely different kettle of fish. Now the move into the factories and the cities became irresisitible.

Unrest was far from unknown in Scotland and, as we've already seen, a social agenda had been a major element in religious protest since the mid-seventeenth century at least. The French Revolution of 1789, with its emphasis on Liberty! Fraternity! and Equality!, impressed many in Scotland, while causing deep disquiet among the ruling elites who tended to develop headaches at the very thought of it. As is so often the case, the lead in organizing revolt was taken not by those who were suffering most from the changing economic conditions but by the more skilled and better-off workers who not only had more to lose but were better able to organize an articulate protest.

The 'Radical War' of 1820 was not the first occasion on which the French Revolution had inspired an attempt to better the conditions of the less well-off, but it was the first to take on the appearance of a mob revolt, as opposed to an appeal from the middle classes. Though tiny in scale, it was suspected that the movement embodied a widespread sympathy for change. As such, it received a typical reaction from the surprised authorities: troops were immediately despatched to Glasgow, the heart of the movement, by a government considerably agitated by social unrest elsewhere in Britain. An attempt to seize the Carron Ironworks near Falkirk, which would have provided the rebels with a nice cache of weaponry, was also thwarted. However, only three men were executed, attesting to the fact that there was considerable support for the rights of the increasingly coherent and articulate working classes among the juries of the industrialized west.

The 'Radical War' did not bring about the kind of change that either the working men themselves, or the middle classes who were sympathetic to electoral reform, desired. However, the failure of violent protest encouraged those who wanted to see political change. The Reform Act (Scotland) of 1832 went some way to acknowledging the transformation of Scottish society which had taken place over the previous century. As well as giving the vote to one in eight adult males (compared with one in 125 before), the Act increased burgh representation, extending it also to the new industrial centres of the west such as Paisley.

This was certainly not enough, and many working class men turned to Chartism, which aimed at much more genuine democratic change (for men), but through the pressure of moral argument, rather than violent protest. Progress was slow but in 1868 a second Reform Act extended the vote to nearly a quarter of a million and in 1884 the Third Reform Act more than doubled that figure. By that time the body of opinion behind change could certainly be described as a popular movement – demonstrations were now commanding the participation of over 250,000 people. The 'Radical War' of 1819-20 may not have been worthy of the name, but it nevertheless marked the tentative beginnings of a genuine working class movement which eventually developed a very clear identity, and social agenda, of its own.

Of far more immediate impact than these tentative moves towards democracy was another major episode in the turbulent history of the church of Scotland. The Disruption of 1843 was ostensibly about who had the ultimate say in the appointment of ministers – lay patrons or the congregation itself. But behind the dramatic events of that year, when nearly an eighth of ministers and around 40% of members walked out of the established presbyterian church of Scotland to set up the Free Church, was the whole issue of what constituted an official national religious institution, and why. By the end of the decade, it had enough financial support to begin a new church building programme, maintain its own schools and run its own affairs. Though the Free Church eventually came to be seen as just as established as the institution it sought to replace, the Disruption reminds us that religion continued to be one of, if not the, most important issue in the lives of Scots of all backgrounds.

Though most Scots still lived in a rural environment even in the first few decades of the nineteenth century, urbanization was one of the main features of the period and it wouldn't be too long till the rural-urban relationship was reversed. As towns and cities increased dramatically in size, the middling sort, now much more vociferous in urban, as opposed to rural, affairs, became the middle classes, while the growing manufacturing

Alongside the rapid industrialization and urbanization of the nineteenth century, an older rural Scotland survived well into the twentieth. Scenes such as peat cutting at Tomintoul (above, 1920s) and ploughing in Dumfries (below, c.1910) were captured on film, testifying against any suggestion that traditional Scotland was suddenly annihilated in the face of new technologies.

Fishing was another traditional Scottish industry that coexisted alongside the new textile and engineering businesses.

But even here, there was increasing concentration in major centres, where mechanization was on the increase. By 1909 half of Scotland's fish was landed at Aberdeen.

classes became identifiable as the working classes. Some cities and towns identified themselves wholeheartedly with the new dynamic industrial transformation; others had more genteel aspirations and preferred to attract the service industries, such as banking and the law, required by a modern economy; some managed to combine both. Glasgow and Edinburgh are the obvious examples of the first two approaches but similar things were happening throughout the lowlands.

As the urban population transformed itself in terms of both sheer size and its composition, what were effectively medieval burghs found themselves bursting at the seams. Edinburgh, crammed uncomfortably within the restrictive bounds of the castle rock, was a classic example of the increasing inability of the old environment to cope. By the later eighteenth century a determined effort was made to do something about the situation. The development of Edinburgh's new town was prompted partly by heightened social pretensions but also by the very practical difficulties of living in the cramped, unsanitary conditions of the old town. In the nineteenth and twentieth centuries Glasgow was held up as the dirty city of Scotland; in the eighteenth Edinburgh was the place that had the middle classes holding their noses in horror.

By 1800 the New Town had become a reality and the elites could finally squeeze themselves out of their old accommodation and relax in the luxurious space of the new. The elegant terraces with their private gardens manifested the values of the Enlightenment in architectural design – order, above all, reigned. Housing developments away from the core areas of the medieval burghs were replicated throughout other Scottish cities, as the middle classes began to find it quite intolerable to continue to live cheek by jowl with their lower class neighbours. Such developments were essential to accommodate not only middle class sensibilities but also the sheer numbers who were now living and working in the cities. The newcomers from the countryside or from elsewhere, like Ireland, were now crammed into increasingly unsanitary conditions.

Glasgow, as the late developer, expanded slowly and judiciously to begin with, but the end result was much the same as hordes of skilled and unskilled workers came looking for work at the dawn of the industrial revolution. The merchant city, which began to be revitalized at the end of the twentieth century, was the very heart of Glasgow in the eighteenth as it grew into the second city of the empire thanks to the tobacco trade. But as the nineteenth century progressed the wealthy industrialists began to realize that the slums of the east end, housing their workers, were far too close for comfort and began to move west. But the cities were not the only environment in which horrific conditions existed. The 1840s were not just disturbed by the Disruption; they were also profoundly affected by famine.

As already mentioned, the years following the arrival of Improvement in the highlands provoked a steady exodus to North America particularly. This voluntary emigration either involved the more affluent members of highland society who could afford to pay their passage across and set themselves up in their new lives, or poorer folk who became indentured servants for a number of years in the New World in exchange for their fare.

Back in Scotland, the vast majority of those whose labour on the land was now surplus to requirements were, in the first instance, moved out of their traditional

Washerwomen in the courtyard of the Saracen's Head, Glasgow, c.1869.

homes to work in new industries which did not interfere with the large-scale farming of cattle or sheep. Kelp (seaweed) was the most obvious example of this process, but the bottom fell out of this market, among others, after 1810. The population was already finding it very difficult to sustain itself on the marginal land now allocated to it even before the arrival of the potato blight destroyed the crop that formed the basic diet there.

The clearances seem, even now, to be a fundamental betrayal of the profound relationship that Scots have always had with their environment. It has been assumed for thousands and thousands of years, rightly or wrongly, that the land's basic function was to sustain the population living on it. That had now changed. Many of the old highland landlords had themselves fallen victim to changing economic circumstances. Their successors were non-resident and culturally far removed from the people on their estates. They felt no sense of traditional responsibility, however diluted. The primary duty of the new landlords was to make their estates viable, and most were agreed that the only way to do that was to get rid of a population that was, even before the 1840s, quite obviously failing to make even the most desperate of ends meet.

The government eventually made an effort to avert the full-scale carnage that affected Ireland so dreadfully thanks to the same potato blight. But this did not alter a general opinion that the best thing to be done with these poor highland communities was to remove them, forcibly if necessary. Emigration was the most obvious solution to the current problem and the interested parties – government, landlords and the wider public – expressed its concern for the individuals involved by paying for their escape to the New World. 16,000 of them had left by 1856, to join the many thousands, including friends and relations, who had already made the trip west.

For those that remained, the pendulum swung back again and conditions improved, partly because, to begin with anyway, the population had been much reduced. However, the Clearances entered the popular consciousness and provided the highlanders with a deep sense of grievance which was eventually transformed into political action in the Crofters Wars of the 1880s. The people of Scotland, whether in the highlands or the lowlands, were no longer prepared to let the interests of the few win out at all costs against the needs of the majority.

The lives of most Scots changed profoundly between 1700 and 1850. Some had become immeasurably richer: as merchants with the skills and ingenuity to take a large share of Britain's increasingly international trade; as industrialists farsighted enough to invest in the new manufacturing industries; and as landowners and larger tenant farmers able to improve the land and its resources for profit, not to sustain its population.

But progress towards a modern economy was not a neat curve into increasing prosperity. Many fell foul of continuing economic slumps, bad investment and changing trends in a rapidly industrializing world. And for many more, these changes, so easily explained as bald facts and figures, eventually meant leaving their homes and traditional ways of life. Particular sections of the working classes managed to better themselves, at least during the early stages of industrial development when the weavers in particular were

A wheelwright seated outside his shop in Smith's Road, Melrose, in 1867, one of innumerable artisans who sought a living in the towns of Victorian Scotland.

By the end of the nineteenth century, Scotland's towns were developing apace; here is a street scene in Irvine.

proud of the work they did in their own homes. Others found themselves with little choice but to endure difficult and dangerous working conditions or face starvation.

Scotland, along with other industrializing nations, had to go through this process in order to earn the wealth which so many of us now enjoy. But there were many besides Robert Burns who must have questioned the suffering that, for those at the bottom of society, was perhaps the most obvious result of the new ideas that property was absolute, that profit was a laudable end in itself, and that the resources of a country were not there to feed, house and clothe its population, but to make a profit for those who were deemed to own it.

Having said that, Scotland had also entered an era when, unusually in the nation's history, it played a leading role on an international stage. Intellectual, as well as commercial life was booming, and confidence and optimism were the order of the day. The union, at last, was fulfilling the promises that its supporters had envisaged and most were prepared to embrace being British without looking too closely at the extent to which economic success was alone responsible for this apparent change of heart. The house of Stewart was now firmly divorced from its people, despite having been the very lynchpin of Scottish identify for much of the previous four hundred years before 1750. It remained to be seen whether Scotland could create and maintain a new identity within Britain, or whether the distinct nature of the once independent kingdom was now surplus to requirements.

TEN

Scotland Renewed

1850 – 2000

If there is one thing that characterizes the most recent past, it is the speed of change. Within one generation in the twentieth century, expectations were transformed from the scarcity conditioned by war and rationing to the rampant consumerism produced by soaring standards of living (for most Scots, anyway) from the 1960s onwards. Technology has been the key to much of that transformation, though perhaps we should pause to consider whether recent innovation has actually changed society to any greater extent than the printing press without which the Reformation might never have happened.

As always, change had its pluses and minuses. In the century after 1850 many Scots continued to experience the depths of poverty and deprivation, as well as the horror of modern warfare. At the same time huge advances were made not just in technology but in the very principles along which society was run, as the country transformed itself from an oligarchy to a democracy. Women found themselves increasingly restricted in what they were permitted to do and be at the beginning of this period and increasingly prominent in almost every aspect of life by the end. Scotland has become a modern, multicultural society, though there is considerable adjustment still to be made before all Scots, whatever their background, can fulfil their potential and enjoy the nation's wealth.

In 1850 Scotland was still undergoing a considerable transformation. The earliest years of Queen Victoria's long reign (1837-1901) coincided with an economic depression, but this soon transformed itself into a boom. We have already witnessed the kinds of technological innovation that led to the industrial revolution, combined with the raw materials and markets available to Britain through its vast empire. By 1850 technology had moved industry on to the kinds of heavy manufacturing for which Scotland became especially renowned. And the railways and steamships were coming, allowing for not only the fast, easy conveyance of passengers but also the quick and regular delivery of goods.

The move away from the cottage industries into factories, engineering works and shipyards marked the final end of an era in terms of the way people controlled their own working environment. But it also marked the beginning of new opportunities for increased prosperity. And with these heavy industries a new working-class culture, fundamentally male-dominated, emerged. The skills of these men provided ships for the world and helped to bring the empire's wealth back to Scotland. But behind every skilled worker laboured large crews of unskilled navvies, whose toil also carved out a new future for Scotland.

Though the Victorians admired men like David Livingstone who moved up through society, they also liked hierarchy more than most – everyone knowing exactly his or her place, the jobs they could have, where they could visit, the people they should meet or even where they could live. Once the middle and upper classes had moved to their own genteel suburbs or new towns, the working classes found themselves left squashed together in their own ghettos. Disgusting unsanitary conditions were not particular to the Victorian era, but as urban populations began to increase dramatically, living conditions became not just unsavoury but downright lethal.

Cholera was the newest disease to strike Scotland, causing havoc on four major occasions between 1830 and 1860 and wiping out up to 10,000 people across the country. The biggest casualties were in the large urban centres, just like plague before it, and Glasgow, with its hideous slums, was hit the worst. Though not as big a killer as typhus, typhoid or tuberculosis, cholera was extremely frightening in its strangeness. It demanded a response.

Victorian attitudes to the terrible problems experienced by those at the bottom of the heap were typically judgmental. Poor relief had long been the responsibility of the church and the Sunday collection was often used to provide essential help to those in the worst situation, at the discretion of the minister and the kirk session. But such small-scale local support was now quite insufficient to deal with the swelling ranks of the urban poor.

Faced with mounting problems, the authorities – predominantly still the church – attempted to deal with the situation by trying to change behaviour. The premise was that anyone failing to provide for his or herself was ultimately responsible through their own immoral or degenerate behaviour. This attitude is not vastly different from how many in the developed world tend to view the catastrophes visited on the developing world. So, instead of arguing for improved housing or pay, for example, the Victorian establishment worked on transforming the poor into model citizens. Only then would they be entitled to any material help. The horror of the workhouse, which Charles Dickens highlighted so movingly in books like *Oliver Twist*, placed those in dire need between a rock and a hard place. Whenever we talk about the incredible achievements of this period, and the wealth that went with it, we must remember this terrible underside.

Not surprisingly the moralizing approach to poverty did little or nothing to improve the situation. But disease eventually did. If cholera had been confined only to the slums then perhaps its terrible impact would also have been interpreted by the authorities as divine retribution for the bad behaviour of the lower classes. But this disease crossed class boundaries and something, therefore, had to be done.

Medical science had made considerable advances in previous centuries, but because penicillin had not yet been discovered, prevention was still regarded as better than cure. As a result, efforts were concentrated on trying to find out how the disease was transmitted and the culprit was found to be water. The Glasgow city fathers therefore proposed an audacious scheme to provide the entire population with fresh running water. Loch Katrine was to be used as a reservoir and its water pumped south to the city. Thousands of men were employed to dig or dynamite a smooth path of tunnels and aqueducts to carry the precious commodity to Glasgow.

Glasgow set the standard for the rest of Scotland, having proved, when cholera struck again in 1866, that such an enterprise would save tens of thousands of lives. The city's

A view of Glasgow's notorious slums in around 1869. By this time efforts were being made to clear the worst areas and create new housing along with parks and effective sewage systems.

A view of the Vennel in Bo'ness shows that it was not just the largest cities that had their slums. This unsanitary eighteenth-century housing had to wait until the 1920s before being cleared.

programme of public investment continued with the creation of various town parks, and not just in the prosperous west end. Having tried to improve the moral standards of Glasgow's poorer citizens, the emphasis switched to promoting their physical wellbeing – and with a healthy body would come a healthy mind.

The Temperance Movement, which in the 1840s attracted tens of thousands of people, including grass-roots, working-class enthusiasts, wwas also part of a continuing moral crusade rooted in a belief in the supposed degeneracy of the poor, though this one was not imposed from above. In reality its biggest impact was to make the pub an environment that no respectable woman could be seen in, an attitude that survived in the odd public house until at least the 1980s. Nevertheless, the Temperance Movement did highlight a public appetite for healthy living, and helped to spark off longer-lasting movements such as the Boys' Brigade.

Underpinning all this achievement was the Empire itself, of which Victoria was the ultimate symbol. Britain could not have industrialized first without the cheap raw materials that its colonies provided and the technologies that continued to keep up with commercial developments. By the 1850s steam ships could travel right across the world and refrigeration finally made it possible to move goods about over long periods of time and distance.

Sauchiehall Street, Glasgow. The white building on the right is Miss Cranston's Tea Room, designed by Charles Rennie Mackintosh in 1903.

And with the growing wealth acquired by the middle classes as well as the nobility, more and more people began to have leisure time to enjoy. Well-groomed ladies could shop in safety in department stores before retiring to the discreet gentility of tea and coffee shops either within the shop itself or in establishments like the famous Miss Cranston's. Department stores displayed the wealth of the Empire, a tangible reminder to its customers of the incredible success story of which they were a part. They also provided an economic lifeline for their female staff, particularly the husbandless – a respectable job outside teaching.

Despite having industrialized and urbanized just as dramatically as elsewhere in the British Isles, the Scots still maintained a largely pragmatic attitude towards the environment that sustained them. The Scottish landscape – the land of the mountain and the flood – became an icon of national identity in the same way as England was idolized as a green and pleasant land. Sir Walter Scott, who gave tourism in the Trossachs a huge boost through his hugely popular *Lady of the Lake*, delighted in the wild beauty of the Scottish landscape rather as William Wordsworth did in the Lake District.

Though Scott was profoundly romantic, he also recognized, as a landowner himself, that nature could be useful. He seems to have made a distinction between perceived 'wild' beauty and the artificial attraction of land made productive through man's wisdom and honest toil. In addition to his fiction, where the untamed landscape (as he saw it) certainly featured as an important backdrop, Sir Walter also wrote treatises on agriculture and forestry. Wordsworth, on the other hand, fought single-mindedly for the landscape to be left in its supposed pristine and native wildness for the enjoyment and

Jean McAlpine's Inn in the Trossachs, pictured c.1910. As tourism took off in the area, this kind of idealized rusticism became very profitable.

moral enrichment of those, like himself, who had the sensibility to appreciate it. But the net result has been very similar – both the Trossachs and the Lake District became well-loved play areas for the large urban populations nearby.

Queen Victoria also played a role in making Scotland popular as a leisure destination. In particular she fell in love with the highlands and helped to create a romantic image for the north that made actually going there attractive. But equally importantly, she seemed to preside over the nation in a manner reminiscent of those far-off days when the monarch had been Scotland's alone. Her decision to buy Balmoral meant above all that Scotland would actually get to see its royal family on a regular basis.

Service in the British army had done wonders for the reputation of the highlander as a brave and loyal soldier. Now the highland landscape would transform itself in the minds of middle and upper class Britons from a hostile and forbidding environment into a playground for the rich. Victoria cannot claim all the credit – many highland landowners had for decades been deliberately promoting deer on their estates in order to encourage shooting them as a commercial enterprise. But the queen's desire for a highland hideaway put a royal seal of approval on the rehabilitation of the area.

And the railways helped to make it all even more possible. It's easy to be disparaging about the train in an era when the car dominates everything and space travel is possible, but there had been nothing else like it before. As well as the employment directly required in order to criss-cross the land with railway track, this revolutionary new form of transport helped to promote tourism. Railway companies worked hand-in-hand with hotel owners (or indeed were run by the same organization) and holiday destinations like Dunoon developed to cater for this new demand for large-scale recreational facilities, creating further jobs for both men and women.

Scotland at the height of Empire was a mass of contradictions. On one level, there seemed to be no limit to possible achievemenst: the Forth Rail Bridge was regarded as a wonder of the modern world; Queen Street Station's vast arch of steel and glass was the biggest single spanned surface in the world; many people, and not just at the top of society, were enjoying more time off, including half-day on a Saturday; one of the deadliest diseases of the modern world had been beaten within a few decades.

And yet working and housing conditions remained appalling. Though the new reservoirs provided clean running water, thousands of people still lived in tiny cramped spaces. And the major manufacturing industries that sustained the Scottish economy were dangerous and difficult – many men lost their lives in building the Forth Rail Bridge alone. Modern Scots have good reason to be thankful for the achievements of their Victorian predecessors, but we should also acknowledge the suffering of so many of them.

Scotland of the twentieth century also witnessed staggering change, and not just in the political sphere that dominated its final decades. One of the biggest themes of the century was the nation's response to the ultimate loss of its heavy manufacturing

The famous Forth Rail Bridge, one of Scotland's proudest achievements.

industries. Those industries had provided not just economic wealth but an important sense of pride, and their loss heralded a crisis of confidence that does not seem to have been evident in earlier changes to Scotland's manufacturing base.

But the turn of the new century soon provided an even more difficult challenge for Scotland and the rest of Europe. The First World War was a struggle for control of the Empire and the Scots had no hesitation in protecting their interests against the Germans. And because they joined up in numbers disproportionately higher than the population, they died in higher numbers too. British generals proved largely unprepared for modern warfare and the stagnant, rotting inhumanity of the trenches has provided far too many horror stories in fact and fiction.

But this war also provided opportunity, as women began to play a higher profile role than they had ever done before. Scotland had its own Florence Nightingales in women like Elsie Inglis and Sophia Jex-Blake, who forced women's health onto the official agenda and played their part in the war effort, despite being officially discouraged. Many women were already better educated, as university places finally became available to them, and now they became increasingly articulate about the unfairness of the almost total denial of public life to their sex, taking to the streets to draw attention to their grievances. In fact the early decades of the century witnessed an upsurge in popular protest.

But the most famous demonstration of discontent took place after the war, when an economic depression swept across the western world. Governments had become tremendously jittery after the successful communist revolution in Russia in 1917; as with the French revolution 130 years earlier large-scale demonstrations, however legitimate the grievances behind them, were viewed with extreme misgiving.

In 1919 100,000 workers took to the streets of Glasgow and the authorities immediately presumed that their worst fears were on the point of being realized. In fact, it had not even occurred to the leaders of the demonstrations to push their numerical advantage into a call for revolution – better conditions continued to be their main focus, especially after their conspicuous success in forcing a rent freeze in 1915. Nevertheless, troops were despatched to George Square. Though the left-wing movement achieved little in 1919, the government's overreaction ensured that Red Clydeside and the man most closely associated with the left-wing movement, John McLean, earned a place in Scottish history and popular culture.

But the deterioration in the economy continued and in 1926 Scotland joined in the national general strike. The miners were some of the hardest hit but the great manufacturing industries as a whole were hugely affected as their markets throughout the world began to dry up. Mass unemployment was a new phenomenon and proved to be the one thing that these tough manual labourers could not cope with. Many of them had suffered deeply in the Great War and now their country seemed to have thrown them on the scrap heap, despite the government's promises.

The Westminster parliament was not completely impervious to the plight of its working (or rather, currently not working) population, nor was it totally unsympathetic to the particular needs of the northern part of Britain. Some recognition of those needs had been

A 1913 demonstration on Glasgow Green in support of Irish transport workers, who were fighting a battle for union recognition.

A more practical response to social inequality was the Co-operative Society, which was very strong in Scotland. This was the scene at the opening of a new branch in 1903.

made in 1885 when a Secretary for Scotland was appointed, though the fact that he was permanently resident in London and was not even admitted to the cabinet until 1892 indicates that his influence was likely to be extremely limited. In 1926, the same year as the general strike, the government acknowledged the seriousness of the situation when it reorganized the office into a full Secretaryship and moved it full-time into St Andrews House in Edinburgh.

Even this important move was likely to be only one step up from window dressing if the appointees themselves proved unequal to the task. But Scotland was fortunate in having two impressive Secretaries of State in the 1930s and 1940s. The first was Walter Elliot, a Conservative, who oversaw the establishment of the Scottish Housing Association to do something about existing dilapidated stock from public funds, and understood the need to diversify away from the heavy manufacturing industries. But perhaps the greatest Secretary of State was Tom Johnson, who served as a Labour member in the Conservative government during the war.

Johnson was a man of tremendous vision. In 1943 he established a hospital scheme some five years before the rest of Britain was given a National Health Service. But his greatest achievement came after the war, when he left government to become head of the Scottish Hydro Electric Board (founded in 1943). This was a deliberate attempt to revitalize Scotland's industrial base, as Elliot had tried to do, but it failed to bring about a large-scale influx of new light industries. However, Johnson's vision of cheap electricity to be accessed equally throughout the country was a huge success, especially in the highlands. These developments are also indicative of an increasing willingness to allow

The cavalcade of trams in this 1920s view of Union Street, Glasgow, were only part of the raft of benefits brought by the increasing supply of electricity in Scotland.

German bombers over Lerwick, 1939. The rising smoke is from a destroyed flying boat.

Scotland to control aspects of its own administration, and they are not the only ones. The Scottish Tourist Board was established in 1945, and the Scottish Office also gained a degree of control over the Forestry Commission, established in 1919 to ensure that Britain maintained a strategic reserve of timber.

But still Scotland was not satisfied. It is difficult to establish any direct cause and effect between many of the long-term and fundamental changes taking place in society and the economy, and shifting attitudes towards the nation's identity and position within the politics of the Union. It would, for example, be rather simplistic to assert that the dissolution of the Empire, out of which Scotland had done so well, led directly to a fundamental questioning of the relationship with England. But a sense of grievance was certainly developing whereby economic difficulties were equated with political disenfranchisement. This was as true in the 1980s as in the 1920s – the poll tax, which applied equally throughout the United Kingdom in the eighties, became a nationalist issue in Scotland, where it was imposed for an extra first year, whereas elsewhere it was hated by many because they regarded it simply as unfair.

The Westminster government, backed up by the Scottish Office in Edinburgh, certainly tried, investing heavily to prop up the failing manufacturing industries of which Ravenscraig was perhaps the most tragic example (the strip mill finally closed in 1993, having been kept in existence beyond its natural life by government subsidies). Some initiatives succeeded dramatically – in petro-chemicals, computers and electronics and, most spectacularly, oil, which transformed the city of Aberdeen from a glorified fish and farmer's market to a modern international industrial centre. In many ways Scotland has proved able to adapt to new economic pressures – its service and financial industries are currently extremely successful and world-renowned. But

Possibly the greatest symbol of the dynamism that was Scotland's heavy industry: the Queen Mary, *fitted out in Clydeside between 1934 and 1936. Her fitting out marked the end of the worst of the Depreesion for Clydeside, while her construction generally marked the apogee of Scottish shipbuilding.*

the loss of its core manufacturing base seemed to strike at the heart of the nation and affects it even today.

Paradoxically, the difficult economic years of the 1930s and '40s also heralded the beginning of a new era of mass entertainment. The movies were extremely popular, providing brief moments of well-earned escapism and familiarizing many Scots with American culture. The social protests of earlier decades bore fruit in, for example, the rights of workers to have a paid annual holiday, and many seaside resorts, such as Rothesay on the Isle of Bute, played host to scores of urbanites coming 'doon the watter' to play in the sand and eat ice cream.

The motor car, too, transformed people's leisure time, as it became increasingly accessible through the average pay packet. From the fifties onwards the whole family could drive out into the countryside, where they might merely indulge in a picnic or else, in more recent decades, take part in sports such as mountaineering and skiing. And with this increased access came a greater concern for the environment in general. 'Ownership' of the countryside now no longer resided purely with the proprietors; the nation had begun to take an interest and express its views on how it should be managed. From access to the hills to the banning of fox hunting, the urban middle classes in particular have forced change.

The 1960s finally heralded an impressive economic upturn as standards of living began to improve dramatically for much of the population. The liberalization of

Once workers obtained the right to an annual holiday, Rothesay saw a dramatic increase in tourism. Here an organ grinder and his monkey entertain passers-by.

Punch and Judy were another Rothesay staple, capable of attracting large crowds.

Broughty Ferry also profited from tourism, albeit in a style very different from today! This photograph from c.1915 shows eight bathing machines being pulled by horses into the sea.

Another effect of the increase in leisure has been the phenomenal growth in sports actvities. Association Football has come a long way since the Motherwell team was photographed in the 1909/10 season.

society, for which the decade has become the byword, affected every class, but perhaps women most of all. With the introduction of the pill, and, in 1976, the legal admission of equality, women were technically free to make their way in the world unencumbered by traditional responsibilities of house and home, if that was what they wanted. Technological innovation had already made their domestic duties less onerous – it's hard to imagine now what life was like before the washing machine and the vacuum cleaner.

Economic independence has certainly followed, and the distinct roles of men and women are now far less clearcut than they have ever been. Indeed, in many ways women seem to have adapted better to the new economic conditions, which place service industries at the heart of the country's economic performance. Inequalities certainly still exist but Scotland is moving on.

Scotland is also no longer a nation of caucasians, with the odd exotic like the 'lady of the meikle lippis' who graced the court of James IV and was celebrated in William Dunbar's poetry. Immigration, not to mention emigration, has always been a part of the nation's history, but the twentieth century has witnessed a considerable increase in the range of ethnic groups settling here. Italians, Poles, Pakistanis, Indians, Chinese and (the largest group) English have all contributed to the nation's wealth and its culture. The fact that some of these groups identify themselves as Scots *and* members of their original societies is no more a contradiction than an American or Australian Scot feeling the pull of the homeland.

Scottish identity has gone through many alterations in the twentieth century, as it has throughout the nation's history. The 1920s inspired members of the Scottish literati, the most influential of whom was Hugh MacDiarmid, to lambast the kitschy tartanized identity which they blamed on Sir Walter Scott, among others. They were looking for an independent identity, not an anglocentric one, whether or not they wanted an independent Scotland. The infamous theft of the Stone of Destiny from Westminster Abbey in 1950 has added another romantic story to rival even Scott's, though the latter would certainly not have approved of the demand for Scottish independence which underpinned the whole escapade. Interestingly, however, the stone's official return to Scotland in 1996 proved that Scotland was no longer willing to accept romance in place of more pragmatic political action– its reception was conspicuously lukewarm.

So where does that leave Scotland now? In the year 2000 this is an interesting question. Since 1999 a parliament has been re-established in Edinburgh, with considerable powers over many domestic matters, more family-friendly working conditions than its Westminster big sister and an impressive 37% female members. Despite a false start in 1979, when a majority voted against devolution, the nation has finally accepted responsibility for some of its own actions. It remains to be seen whether or not this transference of some power away from Westminster has strengthened the union or signed its death knell.

Culturally, also, Scotland has re-established an independent identity on a world stage. The Edinburgh International Festival began the process in the 1960s, though the kind of

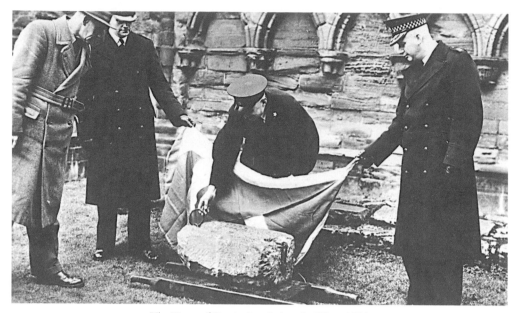

The 'Stone of Destiny' at Arrbroath Abbey, 1951.

artistic achievement promoted there could be found in any major western city. The current popular interest in folk music, which is losing its woolly jumper image, has led to the dramatic success of Glasgow's Celtic Connections festival. The extent to which this is a genuinely 'Scottish' phenomenon is perhaps less important than the fact that it has undoubtedly forged a living tradition out of what could have become a fossilized relic of an older culture.

And we should not be so churlish as to ignore the *Braveheart* phenomenon. The 1995 Hollywood epic depicting the life and terrible times of Sir William Wallace did not *create* a Scottish identity, nor an interest in Scottish history, and the movie says far more about contemporary America than it does about thirteenth century Scotland. But it did make Scotland cool, and finally brought home to the watching world that the nation has a proud history of its own. That is not a bad legacy to carry forward into the twenty-first century.

Ten thousand years of Scottish history encompasses a whole swathe of political, economic, social and cultural arrangements, many of them overlapping and competing at the same time. This history is not about a linear progress from the primitive early tribes to our own sophisticated multicultural society. In the first place, what exactly is progress? For example, so far as many lowland Scots were concerned, trying to force highlanders to abandon their own heritage and language was undoubtedly the way forward (they didn't actually succeed, of course, and many have now adopted a highland heritage as their own), but such an approach is certainly not acceptable today. On the other hand, we can clearly recognize when advances have been made, though we should be careful to admit that these are often measured by the standards of our own time and others in the future may well think differently.

The peoples of prehistoric Scotland had no concept of nationhood or identity similar to our own. But within their predominantly tribal-oriented society, we can still trace changes in the ways in which they organized and viewed themselves over time. A degree of centralization is detectable by the Bronze Age, suggesting that power had passed from elders chosen from the group to a more exclusive form of leadership. This led to an increasing ability to exploit the resources of a given area and create wealth, though the extent to which this was distributed equally among the group probably began to decrease. Material culture became more advanced, and international trade played a greater role in expanding the import and export markets, and cultivating links with elsewhere.

The transition from a tribal society to a kingdom was a slow process lasting hundreds of years. Though the gradual emergence of embryonic nation states was also happening elsewhere in western Europe, 'Scotland' could have remained profoundly uncentralized, effectively a loose confederation of much more focused smaller groups. The Romans can be given credit for providing some of the impetus that made much closer relations among the indigenous peoples absolutely imperative in order to see off the southern invaders. But, ironically enough, hostilities between these increasingly cohesive groups also played their part – whenever there was a peace treaty at the end of a war, there tended to be a marriage between the chiefly families. And so, in time, many ended up related to each other and take-over bids, friendly or otherwise, became increasingly possible.

Alba was Scotland, but only if we are prepared to imagine a kingdom in miniature without many of the regions currently encompassed by the term. Perhaps of more importance than its geographical extent was the fact that the kings of this amalgamated Dal Riatan-Pictish political unit were able to create a unified administration and, finally, identity which began to bind people ever more strongly to the kingdom as well as the king. Having said that, regional identities remained extremely powerful and local politics played a far greater role in the lives of most individuals than the intrigues centred around the royal court.

This basic lack of centralization survived the bitter wars with England which broke out in 1296, not because kingship was weak (though defining what that might mean is difficult) but because it suited the country to do so. However, Scottish identity certainly became more assertive as a result of the struggle for independence, and the protection of the southern border against the Auld Enemy became a fundamental element of Scottish domestic and foreign policy. As an ally of France, the Scots sometimes became embroiled in European politics beyond their needs, but the Auld Alliance did provide Scotland with a measure of protection against England, not to mention an entrée into wider continental society. Though situated on the outer rim of Europe, the Scots were extremely active throughout Christendom, as merchants, soldiers, scholars, diplomats and adventurers.

Medieval Scotland was certainly not in the premier division of European powers, but it was a successful, stable society, even if the effects of harvest failure and disease could not always be alleviated. However, as increasing numbers became literate and the printing press took access to books beyond the clerical and noble elites, Scotland, as elsewhere, began to experience the turbulence associated with fundamental doctrinal challenges to the authority of the church. And thanks to the Reformation, Scotland's relationship with Europe also changed and the centuries of mistrust of England were eased partly by a joint commitment to Protestantism.

Scotland's economic interests, too, were becoming increasingly bound up with England's, especially after the Union of the Crowns in 1603 when the Scottish monarch disappeared, effectively permanently, down to London. Soon many in Scotland could see the benefits which an economic union with England might bring, but it was politics and national security which finally persuaded the southern kingdom of the need to bring its poorer northern neighbour into a more manageable relationship.

The union of 1707 was not popular in Scotland – of that there is no doubt. But, in the longer term, Scotland enjoyed great success as a dynamic and innovative partner in the British Empire. Nevertheless, the price of increasing prosperity was a harsh one for many Scots: the highlands experienced the final brutal subjection of its military power at Culloden in 1746 and the transformation of the agricultural economy meant, ultimately, the removal of tens of thousands of people. The evidence suggests that many would probably rather have stayed, however successful they became elsewhere. Some moved to the expanding cities; others crossed the world to start a new life and create a Scottish diaspora in the New World.

During the eighteenth and nineteenth centuries, Scotland sat at the top table in international affairs, and not just because of the nation's attachment to the primary imperial power, England. The nation's intellectuals and entrepreneurs earned international and enduring reputations for their activities and the Enlightenment was, for many, a Golden Age when being Scottish was a source of great pride.

Economic success continued throughout the Victorian era, but Scotland's dependence on heavy manufacturing industries proved unfortunate in the longer term, as international markets began to dry up in the early twentieth century. The horrors of the World Wars also helped to push forward change in Scottish society as a whole, and the rights of all, of whatever class, gender or race, became a democratic issue.

As the nation's wealth began to rise, increased leisure time provided new economic and cultural opportunities. Popular entertainment, from football to films, took off in a big way. Standards of living continued to improve, providing new freedoms, as well as responsibilities. The nation became more articulate, making increasing demands on government to provide help and support in all aspects of people's lives.

And finally, the Scottish people decided that it was time to bring back a parliament to Scotland. The reasons behind that decision are many and complex, and it could even be argued that, as in 1707, it was only because southern England's interests happened to coincide with constitutional change that the idea was mooted at all. Nevertheless, in contrast to 1978, the Scots also wanted to take an increasing responsibility for domestic decisions. Edinburgh is once more a genuine capital and enjoying the increased attention and attendant economic benefits that follow in the wake of politicians. This is not a resumption of the 1707 parliament. This is a new democratic institution which

A proud member of the growing middle classes at the turn of the twentieth century, A. Neilson stands with his staff outside his Kirkcaldy premises.

hopefully will come more and more to mirror the class, gender and racial mix of modern Scotland.

Where Scotland chooses to go now will be conditioned in part by the nation's past, though it must not be dictated by it. But if one lesson should be learned from history, it is that the crisis of confidence that characterized much of the twentieth century is not intrinsic to the Scottish psyche. The Scots, for most of their history, have been capable of great achievement, while also enduring great suffering. They have much to be proud of.

Further Reading

Prehistoric and Early Scotland (Chapters 1-4)

Ian Armit, *Scotland's Hidden History* (Tempus & Historic Scotland, 1998)

Kevin J. Edwards & Ian B.M. Ralston (eds.), *Scotland: Environment and Archaeology, 8000 BC – AD 1000* (John Wiley & sons, Chichester, 1997)

Sally Foster, *Picts, Gaels and Scots* (Historic Scotland/Batsford, 1996)

Historic Scotland/Canongate series

Bill Finlayson, *Wild Harvesters: The First People in Scotland* (Canongate, 1998)

Gordon Barclay, *Farmers, Temples and Tombs: Scotland in the Neolithic and Early Bronze Age* (Canongate, 1998)

Richard Hingley, *Settlement and Sacrifice: The Later Prehistoric People of Scotland* (Canongate, 1998)

Gordon Maxwell, *A Gathering of Eagles: Scenes from Roman Scotland* (Canongate, 1998)

Ewan Campbell, *Saints and Sea-Kings: The First Kingdom of the Scots* (Canongate, 1999)

Olwyn Owen, *The Sea Road: A Viking Voyage through Scotland* (Canongate, 1999)

Martin Carver, *Surviving in Symbols: A Visit to the Pictish Nation* (Canongate, 1999)

Chris Lowe, *Angels, Fools and Tyrants: Britons and Anglo-Saxons in Southern Scotland* (Canongate, 1999)

Michael Lynch, *Scotland: A New History* (Pimlico, 1992)

Alan McKirdy and Roger Crofts, *Scotland: The Creation of its Natural Landscape. A Landscape Fashioned by Geology* (Scottish Natural Heritage, 1999)

Richard Tipping, 'The form and fate of Scotland's woodlands', in *Proceedings of the Society of Antiquaries of Scotland*, 124 (1994), 1-54.

Medieval Scotland (Chapters 5-7)

G.W.S. Barrow, *Robert Bruce and the Community of the Realm of Scotland* (Edinburgh University Press, 1988)

S. Boardman, *The Early Stewart Kings: Robert II and Robert III, 1371-1406* (Tuckwell Press, 1996)

Dauvit Broun, *The Irish Identity of the Kingdom of the Scots in the twelfth and thirteenth centuries* (Boydell, 1999)

Dauvit Broun, R.J. Finlay and Michael Lynch, *Image and Identity. The Making and Remaking of Scotland Through the Ages* (John Donald, 1998)

E.J. Cowan and R. Andrew McDonald (eds.), *Alba: Celtic Scotland in the Medieval Era*, (Tuckwell Press, 2000)

Michael Lynch, *Scotland: A New History* (Pimlico, 1992)

R. Andrew MacDonald, *The Kingdom of the Isles. Scotland's Western Seaboard, c.1100-c.1336* (Tuckwell Press, 1997)

Fiona J. Watson, *Edward I and Scotland, 1296-1305* (Tuckwell Press, 1998)

Modern Scotland

T.M. Devine, *The Scottish Nation, 1700-2000* (Penguin, 1999)

T.M. Devine and R.J. Finlay (eds.), *Scotland in the Twentieth Century* (Edinburgh University Press, 1996)

R.J. Finlay, *A Partnership for Good? Scottish Politics and the Union since 1980* (John Donald, 1997)

Michael Fry, *Patronage and Principle. A Political History of Modern Scotland* (Aberdeen University Press, 1987)

Christopher Harvie, *No Gods and Precious Few Heroes. Scotland 1914-1980* (Arnold, 1981)

Michael Lynch, *Scotland: A New History* (Pimlico, 1992)

Allan I. Macinnes, *Clanship, Commerce and the House of Stuart, 1603-1788* (Tuckwell Press, 1996)

T.C. Smout, *A History of the Scottish People, 1560-1830* (Fontana Press, 1990)

T.C. Smout, *Nature Contested: Environmental History in Scotland and Northern England since 1600* (Edinburgh University Press, 2000)

Christopher A. Whateley, *Scottish Society, 1707-1830. Beyond Jacobitism, towards industrialisation* (Manchester University Press, 2000)

Maps

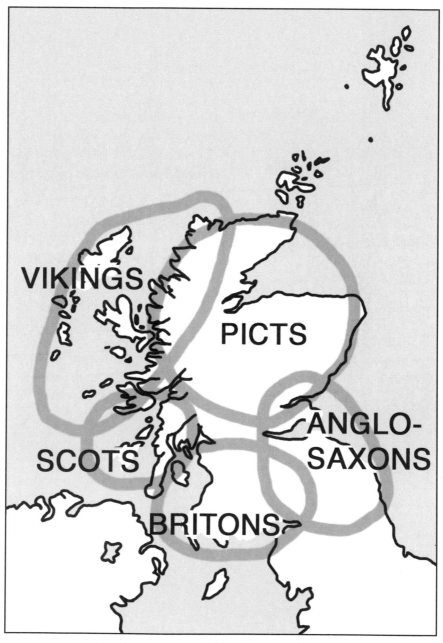

I – Approximate zones of the early peoples of Scotland

Shetland

Orkney

Caithness

Sutherland

Elgin
Inverness

Moray

Skye

ABERDEEN

Atholl

Glencoe

Dundee

Argyll

Perth

Fife
St Andrews

Iona

Inveraray
Kilmartin
Stirling
Dumbarton
Dunfermline
Dunoon
Falkirk
Dunbar
Greenock
GLASGOW
EDINBURGH
Govan
Berwick upon Tweed
Irvine
Lothian
Roxburgh

Galloway
Dumfries

Isle of Man

II – Towns and regions of Scotland

Genealogies

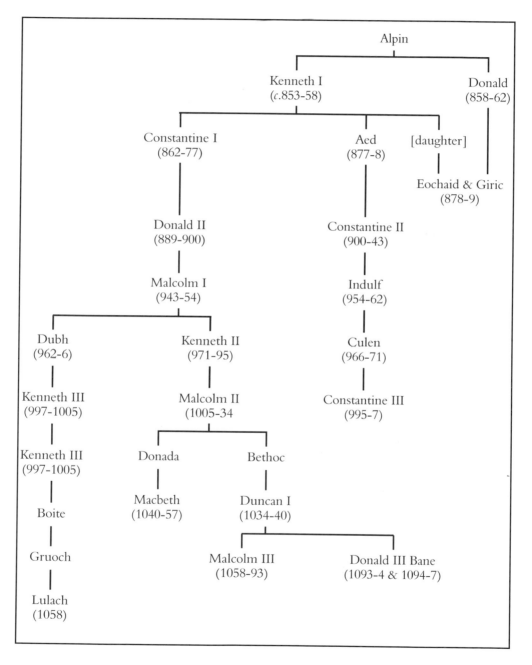

The Scottish succession – c.853-1097

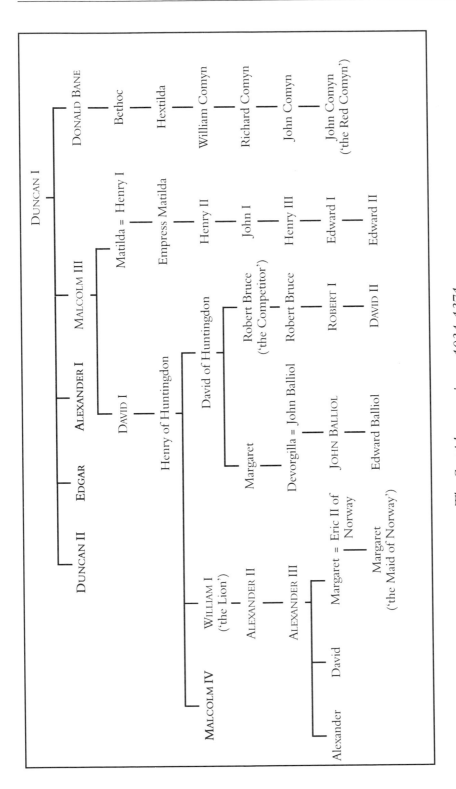

The Scottish succession – 1034-1371

Capitals denote rulers of Scotland

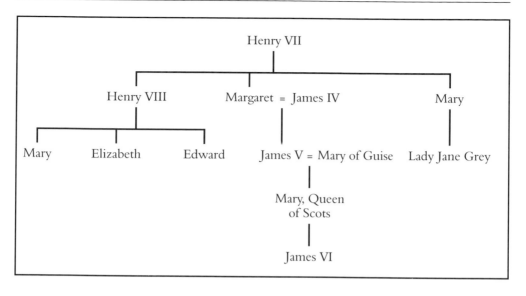

James VI's succession to the English throne

Index